Peter Rabbit™
Baby Knits

Peter Rabbit™
Baby Knits

20 knitting patterns for clothes
and accessories inspired by the
Tales of Beatrix Potter

Debbie Bliss

DAVID & CHARLES
—PUBLISHING—

www.davidandcharles.com

Contents

WELCOME 6

GETTING STARTED 8
How to Read Patterns 8
Reading Charts 11
Safety 11

TOOLS AND MATERIALS 12
Yarns 12
Knitting Needles 14
Other Equipment 16

THE LAYETTES

PETER RABBIT™, FLOPSY, MOPSY & COTTON-TAIL 18
Patchwork Sweater 20
Patchwork Blanket 27
Bunny Ears Beanie 32
Radish Booties 34
Flopsy Capelet 36

JEMIMA PUDDLE-DUCK™ 38
Puddle-Duck Blanket 40
Embroidered Bonnet 48
Jemima Cardigan 50
Duck Beak Booties 56

SQUIRREL NUTKIN™ 58	**TECHNIQUES** 110
Acorn Yoke Sweater 60	Basic Skills 111
Nutkin Jacket 64	Decreases 115
Owl Island Blanket 70	Increases 117
Acorn Hat 78	Intermediate Skills 118
MRS. TIGGY-WINKLE™ 80	Colourwork 120
Mrs. Tiggy-Winkle™ Blanket 82	Creating Texture 122
Gingham Cardigan 87	Seaming 124
Hedgehog Shoes 91	**ABOUT THE AUTHOR** 126
Hedgehog Rattle 94	**ACKNOWLEDGEMENTS** 126
TOM KITTEN™ 96	**SUPPLIERS** 126
Kitten Cardigan 98	**INDEX** 127
Tom's Trousers 102	
Hooded Blanket 104	
Kitten Ears Cap 108	

Welcome

The adventures of Peter Rabbit and his friends have been captivating generations of children for over 120 years, and I couldn't have been more delighted to have been given the opportunity to work on a book of Beatrix Potter-inspired baby designs.

Beatrix Potter's iconic stories and illustrations were so much part of my childhood, have brought joy to every generation since they were first published, and will continue to do so well into the future.

These projects bring alive the beloved characters and motifs for you to knit as part of classic baby garments and accessories, and encapsulate the joy of these enchanting tales.

Designed as heirloom pieces, the patterns in this book are grouped together in five layette sets as I have always loved the idea of small collections with a unifying theme.

I have chosen my favourite characters to be featured — Peter Rabbit, Flopsy, Mopsy and Cotton-tail, Jemima Puddle-Duck, Squirrel Nutkin, Mrs. Tiggy-Winkle, and Tom Kitten, all memorable creatures whether mischievous, curious, or even industrious.

I wanted to inject into the designs the same magical quality found in Beatrix Potter's wonderful illustrations, and for the knits to tell the story through colourwork and stitch.

There is plenty to choose from with designs varying from simple beanie hats to more intricate patterned blankets, so there is something for both the less experienced knitters and also those who prefer a more advanced project. To start you off, I've also included some advice on working with patterns and charts and on the best materials to use.

I hope you will get as much pleasure in knitting the projects as I have in designing them.

Debbie

Getting Started

So many tales begin with once upon a time, but a knitting adventure begins with deciding on your pattern. The layettes are set out in themes by characters, and you can decide to make just one or all of the items in the layette. Here is some guidance on how to begin.

HOW TO READ PATTERNS

For the beginner or inexperienced knitter reading a pattern can be daunting at first. Some patterns will vary depending on the designer or manufacturer, but although some terms and formatting may be different there is a common language throughout.

Read through the pattern first but don't feel too anxious if you come to a part you don't understand. Sometimes patterns only really make sense when you start knitting them. Take care and work the pattern one step at a time, following the instructions one row after another, and referring to the abbreviations as needed.

MATERIALS

Each pattern will say what yarn you need as well as how many balls (see also Tools and Materials). Buy the amount of yarn stated as you may find that the dye lot is no longer available if you buy fewer balls than quoted. The yarn amounts are based on tension (gauge), the number of balls used by the original designer/knitter and are always approximate. Materials will also tell you the sizes of the needles you need and whether you need buttons or other items.

SIZES AND MEASUREMENTS

If a project is available in different sizes for a baby or child, the pattern will usually state the ages, as in 3-6 months, but also the actual measurements of the knit. This is because the ages act as a guideline — in the same way as for adults, children's bodies come in different shapes and sizes so the actual size of the finished project is important. You can get a good idea of what size to knit by measuring an existing baby garment that fits well and then if you prefer make a larger one to account for growth.

When you have chosen the size you want to knit, you need to follow the pattern for that size. The smallest size will be outside the round brackets and the other sizes within the brackets. Some knitters find it helpful to print off or take a copy of the pattern so they can use a highlighter to mark off the size they are making.

TENSION (GAUGE)

Getting the tension (gauge) that is quoted in the pattern is vital if you want to create a garment that has the right measurements and is the same as the pattern you have chosen to knit. A tighter tension will make the project smaller, a looser one will make it larger and liable to stretch.

If you are knitting without a pattern the ball band of the yarn you are using will tell you the needles and tension (gauge) required. If you are knitting from a pattern and the tension differs from that on the ball band, go with the tension quoted in the pattern.

The pattern will tell you how many stitches and rows should fit within 10cm/4in when using the yarn and stitch pattern. Work a tension (gauge) square before you start your project, making it at least 15cm/6in square. When the swatch is completed let it relax for a while, then lay it flat. Using a ruler, measure the number of stitches and rows to 10cm/4in. A ruler is more accurate than a tape measure that can stretch. If the measurements are the same as those quoted in the pattern you can begin knitting, but if they differ try again on a smaller or larger needle — if you have fewer stitches and rows try a smaller needle and if you have more try a larger needle.

Getting Started

ABBREVIATIONS

Knitting instructions use abbreviations to save space and to make reading row instructions easier. These are all the abbreviations used in the patterns, except for special abbreviations that are specific to only one pattern; these are listed on that project's page.

alt	alternate
beg	begin/beginning
cont	continue
cm	centimetres
dec	decrease
DPNs	double-pointed needles
foll	follow/follows/following
g	grams
g st	garter stitch Knit every row when working back and forth. Alternate knit and purl rounds when working in the round.
in	inches
inc	increase
k	knit
kfb	knit into the front and back of next stitch
m	metres
m1	make 1 stitch
mm	millimetres
oz	ounces
p	purl

patt	pattern
psso	pass slip stitch over
rem	remaining
rep	repeat
RS	right side of work
skpo	slip 1, knit 1, pass slip stitch over
s2kpo	slip 2 sts, knit 1, pass slip stitches over
sl1	slip 1 stitch
st/sts	stitch/stitches
st st	stocking stitch (stockinette) Knit on right side rows and purl on wrong side rows. When working in the round, knit every round.
tbl	through back loop
tog	together
WS	wrong side of work
wyif	with yarn held in front
yd	yards
yf	yarn front (yarn over)
*	repeat the instructions before, after or between asterisks as directed
[ ]	repeat the instructions within square brackets as directed

READING CHARTS

In this book I have used both colour and texture charts. One of the advantages of charts is that you can see what the pattern you are making looks like, particularly with colour charts.

Whether texture or colour, a single square represents one stitch horizontally and one row vertically. A key will show you what each coloured square or symbol represents and within the written-out instructions you will be told where to place the chart.

Usually, the first row of a chart is worked on a right side row and read from right to left on right side rows and from left to right on wrong side rows.

Both colour and texture charts are used in the Peter Rabbit Patchwork Sweater and Patchwork Blanket and also in the Squirrel Nutkin Owl Island Blanket.

If a colour pattern is repeated across a row usually only the repeat is charted, with edge stitches each side. This type of chart is used in the Squirrel Nutkin Acorn Yoke Sweater which has a Fair Isle yoke.

Some charts will also show embroidery details to be added once the knitting is complete. These will be mentioned in the finishing instructions. Use the appropriate yarn or embroidery thread (floss) colour as instructed.

SAFETY

It is very important that you make sure that your baby knits are child friendly. Buttons, fasteners and add-ons such as pom-poms and decorative features, like the stem and leaves on the Squirrel Nutkin Acorn Hat, should be sewn on firmly to make sure they don't detach and enter the child's mouth. Cords and ribbons shouldn't be used around the neck.

Tools and Materials

When setting off on your knitting journey, once you've decided on the pattern you don't need much — the right yarn and suitable needles, with some other equipment to lend a helping hand.

YARNS

The yarns I have chosen for the book are specifically made with babies in mind so they are gentle against the skin. Here are the yarns used in the book and a guide to their types and weights.

DEBBIE BLISS BABY CASHMERINO

A lightweight yarn between a 4ply (fingering) and a double knitting (DK).

55% Merino wool, 33% microfibre, 12% cashmere. 125m/137yd per 50g/1¾oz ball. Machine washable.

DEBBIE BLISS ECO BABY WOOL

Sport/5ply weight.

100% wool. 124m/136yd per 50g/1¾oz ball. Machine washable.

WEST YORKSHIRE SPINNERS BO PEEP LUXURY BABY DK

Double knitting (DK) weight.

52% Falkland Islands wool, 48% nylon. 112m/122yd per 50g/1¾oz ball. Machine washable.

WEST YORKSHIRE SPINNERS PURE DK

Double knitting (DK) weight.

100% Falkland Islands wool. 112m/122yd per 50g/1¾oz ball. Hand wash only.

YARN SUBSTITUTIONS

If you do decide to substitute the yarn I have used you will need to do the following to help you decide how many balls you need.

Check the number of metres/yards stated on the ball band on one ball of the yarn used in the design, then multiply by the number of balls quoted in the pattern. This will give you the number of metres/yards needed in total. Divide this amount by the number of metres/yards in one ball of the substitute yarn and you will get an approximate idea of how many balls of the substitute yarn you need to buy. You may want to buy an extra ball just to be safe.

Remember when substituting to use a similar fibre — a cotton instead of a wool will produce a different fabric, which may be less elastic, or using a wool instead of a cotton may mean a subtle stitch pattern may be lost and the springy quality of the fibre cause the garment to pull in.

Even more importantly, choose the same weight of yarn originally used — if you knit a design in a 4ply (fingering) yarn which was originally knitted in a double knitting (DK) yarn your garment will be smaller and have different proportions.

GARMENT CARE

Most of the yarns I have used are machine washable but if using a different yarn from the suggested yarn for a project, check the ball band to see whether it is hand or machine washable and at what temperature it should be washed. If you machine wash your project, dry the knits on an absorbent cloth or towel and pat into shape as they may have become stretched or distorted in the washing machine. If you hand wash your projects, you should dry them in the same way.

KNITTING NEEDLES

There is a large array of knitting needles to choose from but the ones you are more likely to use are straight, circular and double-pointed needles (DPNs).

Most of the patterns in this book use straight needles whilst circular needles are used for the beanie style hats.

STRAIGHT NEEDLES

Knitting needles are available in different materials such as bamboo, steel, aluminium, wood and even milk (actually from casein, a milk protein). The type you choose can depend on the project you are working on or your personal preference. For example, bamboo needles may be easier for beginners to work with because they are less slippery and the stitches less likely to slide off. I often change the needles I use according to the yarn I am using — a sharper point can make working finer yarn easier, particularly with a lace stitch.

Different thicknesses of needles are used for different types of yarn and are sized by the metric or US sizing method. The needle size you use will depend on the weight of the yarn, with a larger needle for thicker yarn and a smaller one for a finer yarn. A standard double knitting (DK) yarn, for example, is usually worked on a 4mm (US 6) needle whilst a chunky yarn is normally knitted using 6mm (US 10) needles.

Needles come in different lengths too. If you have a large number of stitches to cast on you will need a longer needle length. When I am swatching as part of my design work or knitting small garments I prefer to work on shorter needles.

CIRCULAR NEEDLE

This is a plastic or nylon cable with short, straight needle tips at each end. They are used mainly for knitting in the round which avoids a seam. They are particularly useful for projects such as hats or socks that are worked in the round (see for example the Peter Rabbit Bunny Ears Beanie and the Squirrel Nutkin Acorn Hat). You can also use circular needles to work backwards and forwards when you have many stitches, such as on a blanket, shawl, or for picking up the front bands on a cardigan.

I find them particularly useful when I am knitting backwards and forwards while knitting on the go — it helps avoid dropping a needle or elbowing your fellow traveller.

DOUBLE-POINTED NEEDLES (DPNS)

Double-pointed needles have a point at each end and commonly come in sets of four or five. They can be used for working in the round on projects such as socks. Some people prefer working in the round on double-pointed needles rather than on a circular needle.

NEEDLE SIZES

Use this table to convert metric and US sizes, but you may also want to confirm the size of needles you have using a needle gauge (see Other Equipment).

METRIC	US
1.5mm	000
1.75mm	00
2mm	0
2.25mm	1
2.75mm	2
3mm	2-3
3.25mm	3
3.5mm	4
3.75mm	5
4mm	6
4.5mm	7
5mm	8
5.5mm	9
6mm	10
6.5mm	10½
7mm	10½–11
7.5mm	10½–11
8mm	11
9mm	13
10mm	15
12mm	17
16mm	19
19mm	35
25mm	50

Tools and Materials

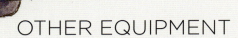

OTHER EQUIPMENT

There are a lot of products available to help the crafter, but my basic list would be as follows.

NEEDLE GAUGE

I have a lot of old knitting needles gifted to me over the years and they tend to have old UK Imperial needle sizes, or the size has rubbed off. A needle gauge is essential for checking the size.

STITCH HOLDERS

These are used to hold a set of stitches separately from the others that are being worked on, such as on a neckband when you are shaping the sides of the neck. A stitch holder that is double ended means that you can work those stitches straight off the holder rather than slipping them back onto a needle.

MARKERS

Stitch markers are attached to a stitch so that you can refer to it later. They are particularly useful to mark off repeats in a stitch pattern.

CABLE NEEDLE

These are used to hold stitches not being used when working cables. A U-shaped or cranked (bent) cable needle is particularly useful to prevent these stitches being dropped when moving them. Use a cable needle that is near to the size of the knitting needles that you are using.

ROW COUNTER

I find a row counter essential as I very quickly lose track of how many rows I have worked, particularly in a complicated stitch pattern.

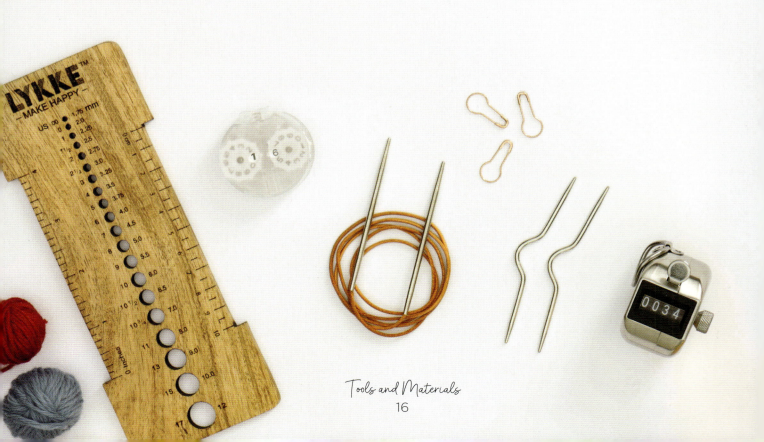

SEWING NEEDLES

When sewing seams, you will need a blunt-tipped or tapestry (darning) needle to ensure that you don't split the knitted stitch when seaming. For the same reasons a sewing needle with a blunt tip is also necessary for Swiss darning/duplicate stitch.

On fabric a sharper pointed needle is used for embroidery, but on the knitted fabric (see for example the Jemima Puddle-Duck Embroidered Bonnet), a blunt-edged needle is used to prevent splitting the stitches below the embroidery.

POM-POM MAKER

After years of making my pom-poms the traditional way with card circles, discovering the pom-pom maker was a revelation. Although not an essential piece of equipment, I use them for children's workshops, hat toppers and decoration on scarves or homeware. They come in different sizes and are reusable.

RULER/TAPE MEASURE

I use a fabric tape measure to check the measurements of my knitted pieces or a finished garment. However when I am measuring my tension (gauge), rather than using a tape that can stretch I use a hard rule to make sure I am getting the most accurate information on the stitches and rows.

SCISSORS

Knitting patterns traditionally use the term "break yarn" but this doesn't mean that you should pull the yarn apart with your hands. Use a pair of sharp scissors instead. Small sharp-pointed scissors are also useful if you want to unpick a seam.

Peter Rabbit™

FLOPSY, MOPSY & COTTON-TAIL

The Tale of Peter Rabbit was first published by Frederick Warne in 1902 and endures as Beatrix Potter's most popular and well-loved tale. It introduces the mischievous Peter Rabbit and his sisters Flopsy, Mopsy and Cotton-tail. Peter's narrow escape from Mr. McGregor's garden after snacking on delicious lettuces and radishes is made all the more memorable by the illustrations of him in his blue jacket and his sisters in their bright red capes as they pick blackberries.

A mixture of colourwork and stitch pattern, this layette for mischievous little bunnies includes a textured patchwork sweater and cot blanket. Snacks are provided for them with radishes and turnips, plus the adorable dress-up items include a bunny-ears beanie, radish-trimmed booties, and a sweet red capelet.

Patchwork Sweater

MEASUREMENTS

TO FIT AGES
0–3   3–6   6–9   9–12 months

FINISHED SIZES
Chest
52   55   62   65 cm
20½   21¾   24½   25½ in

Length to shoulder
24   24   30   30 cm
9½   9½   11¾   11¾ in

Sleeve length
13   15   17   19 cm
5   6   6¾   7½ in

MATERIALS

Yarn quantities are based on average requirements and are therefore approximate.

- 50g/1¾oz balls of Debbie Bliss Baby Cashmerino:
  - 4(4:4:5) balls in Ecru (A)
  - 1 ball in Teddy (B)
  - 1 ball in Mist (C)
  - 1 ball in Ruby (D)
  - 1 ball in Wasabi (E)
- Pair of 3mm (US 2–3) knitting needles
- Pair of 3.25mm (US 3) knitting needles
- 4 small buttons
- Stitch markers
- Stitch holders
- Dark brown embroidery thread (floss) for details
- Small amount of Mink for details
- Cable needle

TENSION

25 sts and 34 rows to 10cm/4in square over st st using 3.25mm (US 3) needles.

SPECIAL ABBREVIATIONS

tw2R – twist 2 right: K into front of 2nd st, k into front of first st, slip sts off needle together.

C4B – cable 4 back: Slip 2 sts onto cable needle and hold to back of work, k2, then k2 from cable needle.

bobble st: K in front, back, front and back of next st, turn, p4, turn, k4, turn, p4, turn, [k2tog] twice, then pass first k2tog over 2nd.

CHART NOTES

Read charts from right to left when working right side rows and left to right when working wrong side rows.

Note that charts three and four begin on a wrong side row.

If preferred colourwork can be worked using Swiss darning/duplicate stitch on completion.

Tip

Having a button shoulder fastening on a baby sweater means it can be easily and comfortably placed over and off the baby's head

CHART ONE

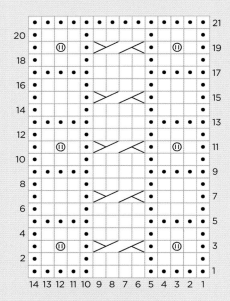

CHART TWO

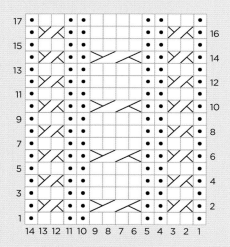

KEY

- ☐ RS: knit / WS: purl
- • RS: purl / WS: knit
- ⋈ C4B
- ⓑ bobble st
- ⋋⋌ tw2R

SWEATER BACK

With 3mm (US 2-3) needles and A, cast on 62(66:74:78) sts.

1st rib row: K2, [p2, k2] to end.

2nd rib row: P2, [k2, p2] to end.

These 2 rows **set** rib.

Work 7 more rows in rib.

Inc row: P1, m1, p30(32:36:38), m1, p30(32:36:38), m1, p1.

65(69:77:81) sts.

Change to 3.25mm (US 3) needles.

1st row: [P1, k1] 1(1:2:2) times, tw2R, work 1st row of chart one, tw2R, [p1, k1] 1(2:3:4) times, work 1st row of chart six, [k1, p1] 1(2:3:4) times, tw2R, work 1st row of chart one, tw2R, [k1, p1] 1(1:2:2) times.

2nd row: [P1, k1] 1(1:2:2) times, p2, work 2nd row of chart one, p2, [p1, k1] 1(2:3:4) times, work 2nd row of chart six, [k1, p1] 1(2:3:4) times, p2, work 2nd row of chart one, p2, [k1, p1] 1(1:2:2) times.

Work 19 rows in patt.

22nd row: [P1, k1] 1(1:2:2) times, p2, work 1st row of chart three, p2, [p1, k1] 1(2:3:4) times, work 22nd row of chart six, [k1, p1] 1(2:3:4) times, p2, work 1st row of chart four, p2, [k1, p1] 1(1:2:2) times.

23rd row: [P1, k1] 1(1:2:2) times, tw2R, work 2nd row of chart four, tw2R, [p1, k1] 1(2:3:4) times, work 23rd row of chart six, [k1, p1] 1(2:3:4) times, tw2R, work 2nd row of chart three, tw2R, [k1, p1] 1(1:2:2) times.

These 2 rows **set** patt and chart placement.

Work 15 rows in patt.

39th row: [P1, k1] 1(1:2:2) times, tw2R, work 1st row of chart one, tw2R, [p1, k1] 1(2:3:4) times, work 39th row of chart six, [k1, p1] 1(2:3:4) times, tw2R, work 1st row of chart one, tw2R, [k1, p1] 1(1:2:2) times.

40th row: [P1, k1] 1(1:2:2) times, p2, work 2nd row of chart one, p2, [p1, k1] 1(2:3:4) times, work 40th row of chart six, [k1, p1] 1(2:3:4) times, p2, work 2nd row of chart one, p2, [k1, p1] 1(1:2:2) times.

These 2 rows **set** patt and chart placement.

Work 19 rows in patt.

60th row: [P1, k1] 1(1:2:2) times, p2, work 1st row of chart four, p2, [p1, k1] 1(2:3:4) times, p21, [k1, p1] 1(2:3:4) times, p2, work 1st row of chart three, p2, [k1, p1] 1(1:2:2) times.

61st row: [P1, k1] 1(1:2:2) times, tw2R, work 2nd row of chart three, tw2R, [p1, k1] 1(2:3:4) times, k21, [k1, p1] 1(2:3:4) times, tw2R, work 2nd row of chart four, tw2R, [k1, p1] 1(1:2:2) times.

These 2 rows **set** patt and chart placement.

Work 15 rows in patt.

3RD AND 4TH SIZES ONLY

77th row: [P1, k1] 1(1:2:2) times, tw2R, work 1st row of chart one, tw2R, [p1, k1] 1(2:3:4) times, k21, [k1, p1] 1(2:3:4) times, tw2R, work 1st row of chart one, tw2R, [k1, p1] 1(1:2:2) times.

78th row: [P1, k1] 1(1:2:2) times, p2, work 2nd row of chart one, p2, [p1, k1] 1(2:3:4) times, p21, [k1, p1] 1(2:3:4) times, p2, work 2nd row of chart one, p2, [k1, p1] 1(1:2:2) times.

These 2 rows **set** patt and chart placement.

Work 18 rows in patt.

ALL SIZES

Cast (bind) off row: Using A, cast (bind) off 20(20:23:24) sts purlwise, patt 25(29:31:33) including st left from cast (bind) off, cast (bind) off rem 20(20:23:24) sts knitwise.

25(29:31:33) sts.

Slip rem sts onto a holder.

SWEATER FRONT

Work as given for back until 20(20:24:24) rows fewer have been worked than on back, ending with a wrong side row.

SHAPE NECK

Next row (right side): Patt 25(25:29:30), turn and leave rem sts on a spare needle.

Work on first set of sts as follows:

Keeping patt correct, dec 1 st at neck edge on every row to 22(22:26:27) sts, then on every foll alt row until 20(20:23:24) sts rem, ending with a wrong side row.

Work 8(8:10:10) rows straight.

K 2 rows.

Buttonhole row (right side): K2(2:4:4), [yf, k2tog, k5] twice, yf, k2tog, k2(2:3:4).

K 1 row.

Cast (bind) off purlwise.

Return to sts on spare needle.

With right side facing, place centre 15(19:19:21) sts on a holder, rejoin yarn and patt to end.

25(25:29:30) sts.

Keeping patt correct, dec 1 st at neck edge on every row to 22(22:26:27) sts, then on every foll alt row until 20(20:23:24) sts rem, ending with a wrong side row.

Work 12(12:14:14) rows straight.

Cast (bind) off.

CHART THREE

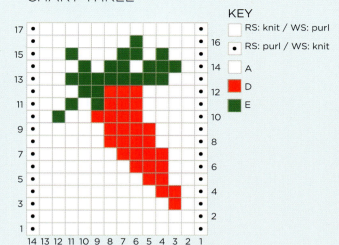

CHART FOUR

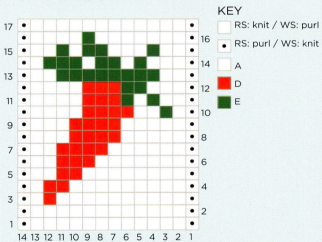

CHART FIVE

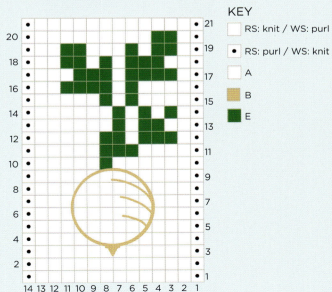

CHART SIX

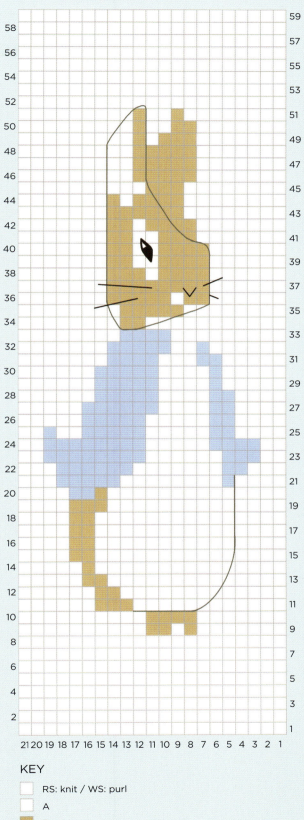

SLEEVES (MAKE 2)

With 3mm (US 2-3) needles and A, cast on 38(42:46:50) sts.

Work in rib as set on back, beg with 1st row, for 6 rows.

Change to 3.25mm (US 3) needles.

Work 4 rows in st st, beginning with a k row.

Inc row: K3, m1, k to last 3 sts, m1, k3.

Work 5 rows in st st, beginning with a p row.

Rep the last 6 rows 3(4:5:6) times and the inc row again.

48(54:60:66) sts.

Cont straight in st st until sleeve measures 13(15:17:19) cm/5(6:6¾:7½)in from cast-on edge, ending with a p row.

Cast (bind) off.

NECKBAND

Join right shoulder seam.

With right side facing and using 3mm (US 2-3) needles and A, pick up and knit 16(16:17:17) sts evenly down left front neck, k15(19:19:21) sts from front neck holder, pick up and knit 16(16:17:17) sts evenly up right front neck, then k25(29:31:33) from back neck holder.

72(80:84:88) sts.

1st row: K3, [p2, k2] to last st, k1.

2nd row: K1, [p2, k2] to last 3 sts, p2, k1.

These 2 rows **set** rib.

Work 2 more rows in rib.

Buttonhole row: Rib to last 3 sts, yf, k2tog, k1.

Work 3 rows in rib.

Cast (bind) off loosely in rib.

MAKING UP

Using Mink and chart for placement, work outline embroidery on chart six.

Using embroidery thread and chart for placement, work face embroidery on chart six.

Measure 9(10.5:12:13) cm/3½(4¼:4¾:5)in down from shoulder seams on front and back and place a marker for armholes. Sew sleeves to armholes between markers, sewing through all three thicknesses at left shoulder. Join side and sleeve seams. Sew on buttons, matching buttonholes.

Patchwork Blanket

MEASUREMENTS

FINISHED SIZE
Length 59cm/23¼in

Width 50cm/19¾in

MATERIALS

Yarn quantities are based on average requirements and are therefore approximate.

- 50g/1¾oz balls of Debbie Bliss Baby Cashmerino:
  - 5 balls in Ecru (A)
  - 1 ball in Teddy (B)
  - 1 ball in Mist (C)
  - 1 ball in Ruby (D)
  - 1 ball in Wasabi (E)
- Pair of 3.25mm (US 3) knitting needles
- Dark brown embroidery thread (floss) for details
- Small amount of Mink for details
- Cable needle
- Optional 3cm/1¼in pom-pom maker

SPECIAL ABBREVIATIONS

tw2R – twist 2 right: K into front of 2nd st, k into front of first st, slip sts off needle together.

C4B – cable 4 back: Slip 2 sts onto cable needle and hold to back of work, k2, then k2 from cable needle.

bobble st: K in front, back, front and back of next st, turn, p4, turn, k4, turn, p4, turn, [k2tog] twice, then pass first k2tog over 2nd.

TENSION

25 sts and 34 rows to 10cm/4in square over st st using 3.25mm (US 3) needles.

CHART NOTES

Read charts from right to left when working right side rows and left to right when working wrong side rows.

Note that charts two, three, four, and eight begin on a wrong side row.

If preferred colourwork can be worked using Swiss darning/duplicate stitch on completion.

BLANKET

With 3.25mm (US 3) needles and A, cast on 126 sts.

1st moss st row: [P1, k1] to end.

2nd moss st row: [K1, p1] to end.

These 2 rows **set** moss st.

Work 6 rows in moss st.

**

1st row: [P1, k1] twice, p1, tw2R, p1, [p1, k1] twice, work 1st row of chart seven, [k1, p1] twice, p1, tw2R, work 1st row of chart one, tw2R, work 1st row of chart five, tw2R, work 1st row of chart one, tw2R, p1, [k1, p1] twice, work 1st row of chart six, [p1, k1] twice, p1, tw2R, p1, [p1, k1] twice.

2nd row: [K1, p1] twice, k1, p2, k1, [k1, p1] twice, work 2nd row of chart six, [p1, k1] twice, k1, p2, work 2nd row of chart one, p2, work 2nd row of chart five, p2, work 2nd row of chart one, p2, k1, [p1, k1] twice, work 2nd row of chart seven, [k1, p1] twice, k1, p2, k1, [k1, p1] twice.

These 2 rows **set** patt and chart placement.

Work 19 rows in patt.

22nd row: [K1, p1] twice, k1, p2, k1, [k1, p1] twice, work 22nd row of chart six, [p1, k1] twice, k1, p2, work 1st row of chart three, p2, work 1st row of chart two, p2, work 1st row of chart four, p2, k1, [p1, k1] twice, work 22nd row of chart seven, [k1, p1] twice, k1, p2, k1, [k1, p1] twice.

23rd row: [P1, k1] twice, p1, tw2R, p1, [p1, k1] twice, work 23rd row of chart seven, [k1, p1] twice, p1, tw2R, work 2nd row of chart four, tw2R, work 2nd row of chart two, tw2R, work 2nd row of chart three, tw2R, p1, [k1, p1] twice, work 23rd row of chart six, [p1, k1] twice, p1, tw2R, p1, [p1, k1] twice.

These 2 rows **set** patt and chart placement.

Work 15 rows in patt.

39th row: [P1, k1] twice, p1, tw2R, p1, [p1, k1] twice, work 39th row of chart seven, [k1, p1] twice, p1, tw2R, work 1st row of chart one, tw2R, work 1st row of chart five, tw2R, work 1st row of chart one, tw2R, p1, [k1, p1] twice, work 39th row of chart six, [p1, k1] twice, p1, tw2R, p1, [p1, k1] twice.

40th row: [K1, p1] twice, k1, p2, k1, [k1, p1] twice, work 40th row of chart six, [p1, k1] twice, k1, p2, work 2nd row of chart one, p2, work 2nd row of chart five, p2, work 2nd row of chart one, p2, k1, [p1, k1] twice, work 40th row of chart seven, [k1, p1] twice, k1, p2, k1, [k1, p1] twice.

These 2 rows **set** patt and chart placement.

Work 19 rows in patt.

***

60th row: [K1, p1] twice, k1, p2, k1, [k1, p1] 14 times, k2, p2, k1, m1 purlwise, [k1, p1] 22 times, k1, p2, k1, [p1, k1] 15 times, p2, k1, [k1, p1] twice.

127 sts.

61st row: [P1, k1] twice, p1, tw2R, p1, [p1, k1] 14 times, p2, tw2R, p2, [k1, p1] 22 times, p1, tw2R, p1, [p1, k1] 15 times, tw2R, p1, [p1, k1] twice.

62nd row: [K1, p1] twice, k1, p2, k1, [k1, p1] 14 times, k2, p2, k1, p1, [k1, p1] 22 times, k1, p2, k1, [p1, k1] 15 times, p2, k1, [k1, p1] twice.

Rep last 2 rows once more.

65th row: [P1, k1] twice, p1, tw2R, p1, skpo, [p1, k1] 13 times, p2, tw2R, p2, [k1, p1] 22 times, p1, tw2R, p1, [k1, p1] 13 times, k1, p2tog, p1, tw2R, p1, [p1, k1] twice.

125 sts.

66th row: [K1, p1] twice, k1, p2, work 1st row of chart three, p2, work 1st row of chart two, p2, k1, [p1, k1] twice, work 1st row of chart eight, [k1, p1] twice, k1, p2, work 1st row of chart two, p2, work 1st row of chart four, p2, k1, [k1, p1] twice.

67th row: [P1, k1] twice, p1, tw2R, work 2nd row of chart four, tw2R, work 2nd row of chart two, tw2R, p1, [p1, k1] twice, work 2nd row of chart eight, [k1, p1] twice, p1, tw2R, work 2nd row of chart two, tw2R, work 2nd row of chart three, tw2R, p1, [p1, k1] twice.

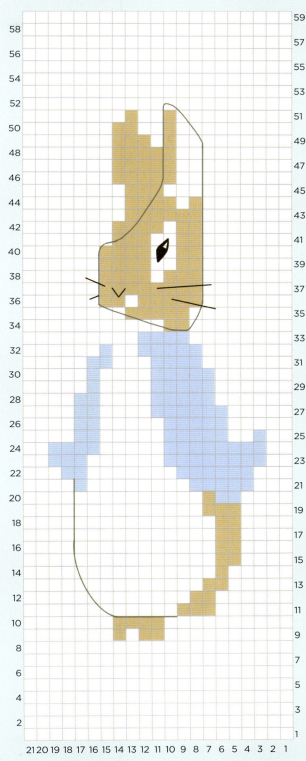

CHART SEVEN

KEY

- RS: knit / WS: purl
- A
- B
- C

These 2 rows **set** patt and chart placement.

Work 15 rows in patt.

83rd row: [P1, k1] twice, p1, tw2R, work 1st row of chart one, tw2R, work 1st row of chart five, tw2R, p1, [p1, k1] twice, work 18th row of chart eight, [k1, p1] twice, p1, tw2R, work 1st row of chart five, tw2R, work 1st row of chart one, tw2R, p1, [p1, k1] twice.

84th row: [K1, p1] twice, k1, p2, work 2nd row of chart one, p2, work 2nd row of chart five, p2, k1, [p1, k1] twice, work 19th row of chart eight, [k1, p1] twice, k1, p2, work 2nd row of chart five, p2, work 2nd row of chart one, p2, k1, [k1, p1] twice.

These 2 rows **set** patt and chart placement.

Work 19 rows in patt.

104th row: [K1, p1] twice, k1, p2, work 1st row of chart three, p2, work 1st row of chart two, p2, k1, [p1, k1] twice, work 39th row of chart eight, [k1, p1] twice, k1, p2, work 1st row of chart two, p2, work 1st row of chart four, p2, k1, [k1, p1] twice.

105th row: [P1, k1] twice, p1, tw2R, work 2nd row of chart four, tw2R, work 2nd row of chart two, tw2R, p1, [p1, k1] twice, work 40th row of chart eight, [k1, p1] twice, p1, tw2R, work 2nd row of chart two, tw2R, work 2nd row of chart three, tw2R, p1, [p1, k1] twice.

These 2 rows **set** patt and chart placement.

Work 15 rows in patt.

121st row: [P1, k1] twice, p1, tw2R, p1, m1, [p1, k1] 14 times, p1, tw2R, p2, [k1, p1] 22 times, p1, tw2R, p1, [k1, p1] 14 times, m1, p1, tw2R, p1, [p1, k1] twice.

127 sts.

122nd row: [K1, p1] twice, k1, p2, k1, [k1, p1] 14 times, k2, p2, [k1, p1] 23 times, k1, p2, k1, [k1, p1] 14 times, k2, p2, k1, [k1, p1] twice.

123rd row: [P1, k1] twice, p1, tw2R, [p1, k1] 15 times, p1, tw2R, p2, [k1, p1] 22 times, p1, tw2R, p1, [k1, p1] 15 times, tw2R, p1, [p1, k1] twice.

Rep last 2 rows once more.

126th row: [K1, p1] twice, k1, p2, k1, [k1, p1] 14 times, k2, p2, k1, k2tog, [p1, k1] 22 times, p2, k2, [p1, k1] 14 times, k1, p2, k1, [k1, p1] twice.

126 sts.

Rep from ** to *** once.

Work 8 rows in moss st.

Cast (bind) off.

TO FINISH

Using Mink and chart for placement, work outline embroidery on charts six, seven and eight.

Using embroidery thread and chart for placement, work face embroidery on charts six, seven, and eight.

Using B and chart for placement, work outline embroidery on chart five.

Using A, make four pom-poms and attach to each corner of the blanket.

Bunny Ears Beanie

MEASUREMENTS

TO FIT AGES
0-3   3-6   6-12 months

TENSION

24 sts and 48 rounds to 10cm/4in square over g st using 3.25mm (US 3) needles.

SPECIAL ABBREVIATIONS

kfbf: Knit into the front, back and front of next stitch to increase two stitches.

MATERIALS

Yarn quantities are based on average requirements and are therefore approximate.

- 50g/1¾oz balls of Debbie Bliss Baby Cashmerino:
    - 2 balls in Teddy (A)
    - 1 ball in Mist (B)
- Pair of 3mm (US 2-3) knitting needles
- 3.25mm (US 3) circular needle, 30cm/12in long
- A set of 3.25mm (US 3) double-pointed needles (DPNs)
- Stitch marker

Tip

Make sure to attach the ears very firmly to the hat

HAT

With 3.25mm (US 3) circular needle and B, cast on 83(91:99) sts.

Join to work in the round, being careful not to twist stitches, place marker for beg of round.

Work 14 rounds in st st (k every round).

Break off B.

Join A.

1st round: K to end.

2nd round: P to end.

These 2 rounds **set** g st.

Cont in g st for a further 28(38:48) rounds, hat should measure 6(8:10) cm/2¼(3¼:4)in from beg of g st, ending with a p round.

SHAPE CROWN

Change to 3.25mm (US 3) DPNs when stitch count becomes too small for your circular needle.

1st round: K10(11:12), [s2kpo, k17(19:21)] 3 times, s2kpo, k10(11:12).

75(83:91) sts.

Work 3 rounds in g st.

5th round: K9(10:11), [s2kpo, k15(17:19)] 3 times, s2kpo, k9(10:11).

67(75:83) sts.

Work 3 rounds in g st.

9th round: K8(9:10), [s2kpo, k13(15:17)] 3 times, s2kpo, k8(9:10).

59(67:75) sts.

Work 3 rounds in g st.

13th round: K7(8:9), [s2kpo, k11(13:15)] 3 times, s2kpo, k7(8:9).

51(59:67) sts.

P 1 round.

15th round: K6(7:8), [s2kpo, k9(11:13)] 3 times, s2kpo, k6(7:8).

43(51:59) sts.

P 1 round.

17th round: K5(6:7), [s2kpo, k7(9:11)] 3 times, s2kpo, k5(6:7).

35(43:51) sts.

P 1 round.

19th round: K4(5:6), [s2kpo, k5(7:9)] 3 times, s2kpo, k4(5:6).

P 1 round.

27(35:43) sts.

2ND AND 3RD SIZES ONLY

21st round: K-(4:5), [s2kpo, k-(5:7)] 3 times, s2kpo, k-(4:5).

-(27:35) sts.

P 1 round.

3RD SIZE ONLY

23rd round: K-(-:4), [s2kpo, k-(-:5)] 3 times, s2kpo, k-(-:4).

-(-:27) sts.

P 1 round.

ALL SIZES

Next round: K1, k2tog, [s2kpo] to last 3 sts, skpo, k1.

11 sts.

Next round: K2, [k2tog] 4 times, k1.

7 sts.

Leaving a long end, break yarn and thread through rem sts, pull up and secure.

EARS (MAKE 2)

With 3mm (US 2-3) needles and A, cast on 1 st.

1st row: Kfbf.

3 sts.

2nd row and every even row: K to end.

3rd row: K1, kfbf, k1.

5 sts.

5th row: K2, kfbf, k2.

7 sts.

7th row: K3, kfbf, k3.

9 sts.

9th row: K4, kfbf, k4.

11 sts.

11th row: K5, kfbf, k5.

13 sts.

13th row: K6, kfbf, k6.

15 sts.

K 75 rows.

89th row: [Sl1, k2tog, psso] 5 times.

5 sts.

Leaving a long end, break yarn and thread through rem sts, pull up and secure.

TO FINISH

Join ears to either side of hat, approximately 12 rounds below brim.

Radish Booties

MEASUREMENTS

TO FIT AGES
0-3   3-6 months

MATERIALS

Yarn quantities are based on average requirements and are therefore approximate.

- 50g/1¾oz balls of Debbie Bliss Baby Cashmerino:
  - 1 ball in Mist (A)
  - 1 ball in Teddy (B)
  - 1 ball in Ecru (C)
  - Small amount of Ruby (D) and Wasabi (E) for radishes

0-3 MONTHS
- 2 x 2.75mm (US 2) double-pointed needles (DPNs)

3-6 MONTHS
- 2 x 3mm (US 2-3) double-pointed needles (DPNs)

BOTH SIZES
- Pair of 2.75mm (US 2) knitting needles for radishes
- 3mm (US D-3) crochet hook
- Stitch holder

SPECIAL ABBREVIATIONS

k1B: Knit 1 st (or number indicated) in yarn B (or other colour indicated).

PATTERN NOTE

A larger needle size is used for the larger booties but instructions remain the same for both sizes.

TENSION

28 sts and 50 rows to 10cm/4in over g st using 2.75mm (US 2) needles.

26 sts and 48 rows to 10cm/4in over g st using 3mm (US 2-3) needles.

BOOTIES (MAKE 2)

With 2.75mm (US 2) or 3mm (US 2-3) DPNs and A, cast on 18 sts (for first half of cuff) and k 16 rows.

Break yarn and leave sts on a holder.

Rep from * to * for second half of cuff.

JOIN CUFF HALVES

Change to B.

Next row: [K1, p1] 9 times across second half of cuff, then [k1, p1] 9 times across first half of cuff.

36 sts.

Next row: [K1, p1] to end.

Rep the last row 6 times more.

SHAPE INSTEP

Next row (right side): K13B, join C but do not break off B, k10C, turn.

Using C, work as follows.

Next row: K10, turn.

Work 24 rows on centre 10 sts.

Next row: K1, skpo, k4, k2tog, k1.

8 sts.

K 1 row.

Break yarn.

With right side facing and B, using yarn left at base of instep, pick up and knit 13 sts evenly along side of instep, k across centre 8 sts, then pick up and knit 13 sts evenly along other side of instep, k rem 13 sts.

60 sts.

K 11 rows.

Work 7 rows in st st, beginning with a k row.

Next row: [P next st tog with corresponding st 7 rows below] to end.

Break yarn.

SHAPE SOLE

Next row: Slip first 25 sts onto right hand needle, rejoin B and k10 sts, turn.

Next row: K9, k2tog, turn.

Rep last row until 20 sts rem, then k to end.

Cast (bind) off.

MAKING UP

Join back seam. With back seam to centre of cast (bind) off, join heel seam.

RADISHES (MAKE 4)

With 2.75mm (US 2) needles and D, cast on 5 sts.

1st row: [Kfb] 5 times.

10 sts.

Work 5 rows in st st, beginning with a p row.

7th row: [K2tog] 5 times.

5 sts.

8th row: P to end.

9th row: K2tog, k1, k2tog.

3 sts.

Leaving a long end, break yarn and thread through rem sts, pull up and secure. Join side seam.

Tip

Always make sure that the cords do not become detached from the booties

With a small amount of E and tapestry (darning) needle, make 3 chain leaves at top of radish as follows:

Join yarn and make a loop, thread yarn through loop. Working into loop just made cont in the same way until chain measures 2cm/¾in, fasten off.

TO FINISH

With crochet hook and B, make two 30cm/11¾in crochet chains for cords. Thread through the rib starting and ending either side of the centre stitch. Sew a radish to each end of crochet cords.

Flopsy Capelet

MEASUREMENTS

TO FIT AGES
0–3   3–6   6–12 months

FINISHED SIZES
Chest

50	58	66 cm
19¾	22¾	26 in

Length

19	22	24 cm
7½	8¾	9½ in

MATERIALS

Yarn quantities are based on average requirements and are therefore approximate.

- 50g/1¾oz balls of Debbie Bliss Cashmerino DK:
  - 1(2:2) balls in Ruby
- Pair of 4mm (US 6) knitting needles
- 1 button

TENSION

22 sts and 30 rows to 10cm/4in square over st st using 4mm (US 6) needles.

SPECIAL ABBREVIATIONS

wrap 1: On a k side row yarn to front, slip next st onto right hand needle, yarn to back, slip st back onto left hand needle, when working across the wrapped st on the next row, work the wrapped st and the wrapping loop tog as one st.

CAPELET

With 4mm (US 6) needles, cast on 114(132:150) sts.

K 6 rows.

1st row: K to end.

2nd row: K4, p to last 4 sts, k4.

These 2 rows **set** st st with g st edging and are repeated throughout.

Work 10 rows straight in patt.

13th row: K8(10:12), [skpo, k5(6:7)] 6 times, skpo, k10(12:14), [k2tog, k5(6:7)] 6 times, k2tog, k8(10:12).

100(118:136) sts.

Work 7 rows straight in patt.

21st row: K8(10:12), [skpo, k4(5:6)] 6 times, skpo, k8(10:12), [k2tog, k4(5:6)] 6 times, k2tog, k8(10:12).

86(104:122) sts.

Work 9 rows straight in patt.

31st row: K8(10:12), [skpo, k3(4:5)] 6 times, skpo, k6(8:10), [k2tog, k3(4:5)] 6 times, k2tog, k8(10:12).

72(90:108) sts.

Work 9 rows straight in patt.

2ND AND 3RD SIZES ONLY

41st row: K-(10:12), [skpo, k-(3:4)] 6 times, skpo, k-(6:8), [k2tog, k-(3:4)] 6 times, k2tog, k-(10:12).

-(76:94) sts.

Work 7 rows straight in patt.

3RD SIZE ONLY

49st row: K-(-:12), [skpo, k-(-:3)] 6 times, skpo, k-(-:6), [k2tog, k-(-:3)] 6 times, k2tog, k-(-:12).

-(-:80) sts.

Work 7 rows straight in patt.

ALL SIZES

NECKBAND

K 2 rows.

Next 2 rows: K to last 15 sts, wrap 1, turn.

Next 2 rows: K to last 14 sts, wrap 1, turn.

Next 2 rows: K to last 13 sts, wrap 1, turn.

Next 2 rows: K to last 12 sts, wrap 1, turn.

Next 2 rows: K to last 11 sts, wrap 1, turn.

Next row: K to end.

Next row: K to last 4 sts, yf, k2tog, k2.

K 3 rows.

Cast (bind) off loosely knitwise.

TO FINISH

Sew on button, matching buttonhole.

Jemima Puddle-Duck™

Keen to safely hatch her eggs, Jemima finds a perfect spot amongst tall foxgloves until a charming gentleman fox persuades her to nest on feathers at his house. He sends the unsuspecting duck to collect herbs for stuffing for his next meal. Luckily farm dog Kep sees through the fox's plan and rescues Jemima.

On the blanket Jemima takes centre stage surrounded by her ducklings and foxgloves. The floral theme carries on in a sweet, embroidered bonnet, and on the classic cardigan Jemima is watching over her ducklings. Cute duckling booties complete the layette.

Puddle-Duck Blanket

MEASUREMENTS

FINISHED SIZE
Length 56cm/22in

Width 44cm/17¼in

MATERIALS

Yarn quantities are based on average requirements and are therefore approximate.

- 50g/1¾oz balls of Debbie Bliss Baby Cashmerino:
    - 5 balls in Ecru (A)
    - 1 ball in Rose Pink (B)
    - 1 ball in Baby Blue (C)
    - 1 ball in Sienna (D)
    - 1 ball in Acid Yellow (E)
    - 1 ball in Wasabi (F)
- Pair of 3mm (US 2-3) knitting needles
- Pair of 3.25mm (US 3) knitting needles
- Dark brown embroidery thread (floss) for details

TENSION

25 sts and 34 rows to 10cm/4in square over st st using 3.25mm (US 3) needles.

CHART NOTES

Because of the style of the motifs I have used Swiss darning/duplicate stitch and embroidery on completion of the blanket, but you can use the Fair Isle and intarsia methods if you prefer to knit the duck and foxglove motifs as you go.

Tip

Charts one and two are large and split across the following pages. To help work them more easily, you may want to photocopy both parts of each chart and join them to make the chart continuous

CHART ONE

KEY

- RS: knit / WS: purl
- A
- B
- C
- D
- E
- F

45

BLANKET

With 3.25mm (US 3) needles and A, cast on 91 sts.

Moss st row: K1, [p1, k1] to end.

This row **sets** moss st.

Work a further 9 rows in moss st.

PANEL ONE

Work 50 rows in st st, working 1st–50th rows of chart one, beginning with a k row.

Work 10 rows in moss stitch.

PANEL TWO

Work 50 rows in st st, working 1st–50th rows of chart two, beginning with a k row.

Work 10 rows in moss stitch.

PANEL THREE

Work 50 rows in st st, working 1st–50th rows of chart one, beginning with a k row.

Work 10 rows in moss stitch.

Cast (bind) off.

RIGHT SIDE EDGING

With right side facing, using 3.25mm (US 3) needles and A, pick up and knit 133 sts evenly up right side edge of blanket.

Moss st row: K1, [p1, k1] to end.

This row **sets** moss st.

Work a further 9 rows in moss st.

Change to 3mm (US 2-3) needles.

K 2 rows.

Cast (bind) off knitwise.

LEFT SIDE EDGING

With right side facing, using 3.25mm (US 3) needles and A, pick up and knit 133 sts evenly down left side edge of blanket.

Moss st row: K1, [p1, k1] to end.

This row **sets** moss st.

Work a further 9 rows in moss st.

Change to 3mm (US 2-3) needles.

K 2 rows.

Cast (bind) off knitwise.

LOWER EDGE BORDER

With right side facing, using 3mm (US 2-3) needles and A, pick up and knit 99 sts evenly along left side edging, along cast-on row and along right side edging.

K 2 rows.

Cast (bind) off knitwise.

UPPER EDGE BORDER

With right side facing, using 3mm (US 2-3) needles and A, pick up and knit 99 sts evenly along right side edging, along cast-off row and along left side edging.

K 2 rows.

Cast (bind) off knitwise.

TO FINISH

Working from chart one, add design to panel one and panel three of blanket by working Swiss darning/duplicate stitch and embroidery.

Working from chart two, add design to panel two of blanket by working Swiss darning/duplicate stitch and embroidery, including body outline for Jemima.

Embroidered Bonnet

MEASUREMENTS

TO FIT AGES
0-3   3-6   6-12 months

TENSION

25 sts and 34 rows to 10cm/4in square over st st using 3.25mm (US 3) needles.

MATERIALS

Yarn quantities are based on average requirements and are therefore approximate.

- 50g/1¾oz balls of Debbie Bliss Baby Cashmerino:
    - 1(1:2) balls in Rose Pink (A)
    - Small amounts in Ecru, Wasabi, Acid Yellow and Baby Blue for embroidery
- Pair of 3mm (US 2-3) knitting needles
- Pair of 3.25mm (US 3) knitting needles

BONNET

With 3mm (US 2-3) needles and A, cast on 69(75:81) sts.

K 5 rows.

Change to 3.25mm (US 3) needles.

Cont in st st, beginning with a k row, for 38(40:42) rows.

SHAPE BACK

Next row: K3, [k2tog, k4] to end.

58(63:68) sts.

Next row: P to end.

Next row: K2, [k2tog, k3] to last st, k1.

47(51:55) sts.

Next row: P to end.

Next row: K2, [k2tog, k2] to last st, k1.

36(39:42) sts.

Next row: P to end.

Next row: [K1, K2tog] to end.

24(26:28) sts.

Next row: P to end.

Next row: [K2tog] to end.

12(13:14) sts.

Next row: P0(1:0), [p2tog] to end.

6(7:7) sts.

Leaving a long end, break yarn and thread through rem sts, pull up and secure.

EDGING

Join back seam from fasten-off edge to beg of shape back.

With right side facing, using 3mm (US 2-3) needles, pick up and knit 29(30:32) sts along each side edge of bonnet.

58(60:64) sts.

K 5 rows.

Cast (bind) off knitwise.

TO FINISH

Using photograph as a guide for placement and with small amounts of Ecru, Wasabi, Acid Yellow and Baby Blue, embroider design, using embroidery diagram for reference, onto left side edge of bonnet.

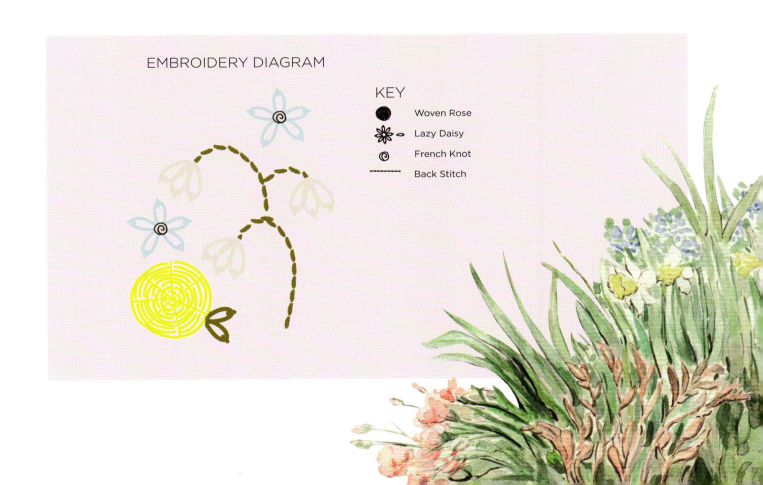

Jemima Cardigan

MEASUREMENTS

TO FIT AGES
0–3 3–6 6–9 9–12 months

FINISHED SIZES
Chest
50 54 58 62 cm
19¾ 21¼ 22¾ 24½ in

Length to shoulder
24 26 28 30 cm
9½ 10¼ 11 11¾ in

Sleeve length
13 15 17 19 cm
5 6 6¾ 7½ in

MATERIALS

Yarn quantities are based on average requirements and are therefore approximate.

- 50g/1¾oz balls of Debbie Bliss Baby Cashmerino:
  - 3(3:4:4) balls Wasabi (A)
  - 1 ball in Rose Pink (B)
  - 1 ball in Baby Blue (C)
  - 1 ball in Sienna (D)
  - 1 ball in Acid Yellow (E)
  - 1 ball in Ecru (F)
- Pair of 3mm (US 2-3) knitting needles
- Pair of 3.25mm (US 3) knitting needles
- 6 buttons
- Stitch markers
- Stitch holders
- Dark brown embroidery thread (floss) for details

TENSION

25 sts and 34 rows to 10cm/4in square over st st using 3.25mm (US 3) needles.

SPECIAL ABBREVIATIONS

k1A: Knit 1 st (or number indicated) in yarn A (or other colour indicated).

CHART NOTES

Read charts from right to left when knitting across chart sts and from left to right when purling across chart sts.

If preferred colourwork can be worked using Swiss darning/duplicate stitch on completion.

CARDIGAN BACK

With 3mm (US 2-3) needles and A, cast on 63(67:73:77) sts.

1st rib row (right side): K1, [p1, k1] to end.

2nd rib row: P1, [k1, p1] to end.

These 2 rows **set** rib.

Work 3 more rows in rib.

P 1 row.

Change to 3.25mm (US 3) needles.

Cont in st st (throughout), beginning with a k row, until back measures 24(26:28:30) cm/9½(10¼:11:11¾)in from cast-on edge, ending with a p row.

SHAPE SHOULDERS

Cast (bind) off 6(6:7:7) sts at beg of next 4 rows and 5(6:7:8) sts at beg of foll 2 rows.

Leave rem 29(31:31:33) sts on a holder.

CHART ONE

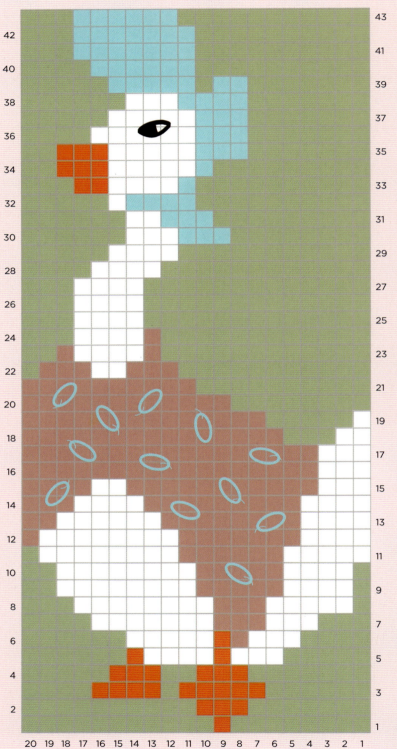

KEY

- RS: knit / WS: purl
- A
- B
- C
- D
- F

52

LEFT FRONT

With 3mm (US 2-3) needles and A cast on 30(32:34:36) sts.

Rib row: [K1, p1] to end.

This row **sets** rib.

Work 4 more rows in rib.

3RD AND 4TH SIZES ONLY

Next row: P to last st, m1, p1.

-(-:35:37) sts.

1ST AND 2ND SIZES ONLY

P 1 row.

ALL SIZES

Change to 3.25mm (US 3) needles.

Work 4 rows in st st, beginning with a k row.

PLACE CHART ONE

1st row: K5(6:8:9)A, work across 1st row of chart one, k5(6:7:8)A.

2nd row: P5(6:7:8)A, work across 2nd row of chart one, P5(6:8:9)A.

These 2 rows **set** chart.

Work 3rd–43rd rows of chart one.

Cont in st st in A only until 12 rows fewer have been worked than on back to shoulder shaping, ending with right side facing for next row.

SHAPE NECK

Next row: Patt to last 8(9:10:11) sts, leave these sts on a holder, turn and work on rem 22(23:25:26) sts for side of neck.

Next row: Patt to end.

Next row: Patt to last 2 sts, skpo.

Rep the last 2 rows four times more.

17(18:20:21) sts.

Patt 1 row.

SHAPE SHOULDER

Cast (bind) off 6(6:7:7) sts at beg of next and foll right side row.

5(6:6:7) sts.

Work 1 row.

Cast (bind) off rem 5(6:6:7) sts.

RIGHT FRONT

With 3mm (US 2-3) needles and A, cast on 30(32:34:36) sts.

Rib row: [P1, k1] to end.

This row **sets** rib.

Work 4 more rows in rib.

3RD AND 4TH SIZES ONLY

Next row: P1, m1, p to end.

-(-:35:37) sts.

1ST AND 2ND SIZES ONLY

P 1 row.

ALL SIZES

Change to 3.25mm (US 3) needles.

Work 6 rows in st st, beginning with a k row.

PLACE CHART TWO

1st row: K3(4:5:6)A, work across 1st row of chart two, k2(3:5:6)A.

2nd row: P2(3:5:6)A, work across 2nd row of chart two, p3(4:5:6)A.

These 2 rows **set** chart.

Work 3rd–14th rows of chart two.

Cont in st st in A only until 12 rows fewer have been worked than on back to shoulder shaping, ending with right side facing for next row.

SHAPE NECK

Next row: K8(9:10:11) sts, leave these sts on a holder, k to end.

22(23:25:26) sts.

Next row: Patt to end.

Next row: K2tog, patt to end.

Rep the last 2 rows four times more.

17(18:20:21) sts.

Work 2 rows.

SHAPE SHOULDER

Cast (bind) off 6(6:7:7) sts at beg of next and foll wrong side row.

5(6:6:7) sts.

Work 1 row.

Cast (bind) off rem 5(6:6:7) sts.

SLEEVES (MAKE 2)

With 3mm (US 2-3) needles and A, cast on 39(41:43:45) sts.

1st rib row (right side): K1, [p1, k1] to end.

2nd rib row: P1, [k1, p1] to end.

These 2 rows **set** rib.

Work 3 more rows in rib.

P 1 row.

Change to 3.25mm (US 3) needles and cont in st st (throughout) as follows.

Work 4 rows straight, beginning with a k row.

Inc row: K3, m1, k to last 3 sts, m1, k3.

Work 5 rows in st st patt.

Rep the last 6 rows 4(5:6:7) times and the inc row again.

51(55:59:63) sts.

Cont straight until sleeve measures 13(15:17:19) cm/5(6:6¾:7½)in from cast-on edge, ending with a p row.

Cast (bind) off.

MAKING UP

Join shoulder seams.

NECKBAND

With right side facing, using 3mm (US 2-3) needles and A slip 8(9:10:11) sts on right front neck holder onto right hand needle, rejoin yarn and pick up and knit 10 sts up right front neck, k29(31:31:33) sts from back neck holder, pick up and knit 10 sts down left side of front neck, k8(9:10:11) sts from left front holder.

65(69:71:75) sts.

1st rib row: K1, [p1, k1] to end.

2nd rib row: P1, [k1, p1] to end.

These 2 rows **set** rib.

Work 3 more rows in rib.

Cast (bind) off in rib.

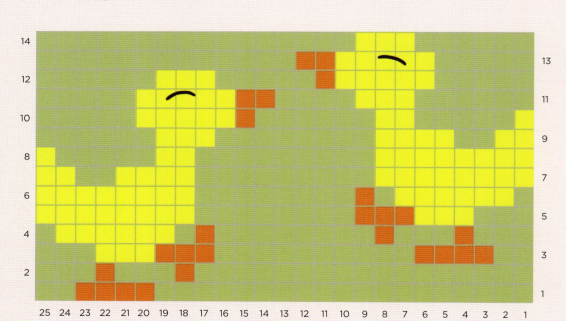

CHART TWO

KEY
- RS: knit / WS: purl
- A
- D
- E

BUTTON BAND

With 3mm (US 2-3) needles, right side facing and A, pick up and knit 55(61:65:71) sts along left front edge.

1st rib row: P1, [k1, p1] to end.

2nd rib row: K1, [p1, k1] to end.

These 2 rows **set** rib.

Work 4 more rows in rib.

Cast (bind) off in rib.

BUTTONHOLE BAND

With 3mm (US 2-3) needles, right side facing and A, pick up and knit 55(61:65:71) sts along right front edge.

1st rib row: P1, [k1, p1] to end.

2nd rib row: K1, [p1, k1] to end.

These 2 rows **set** rib.

Work 1 more row in rib.

Buttonhole row: Rib 4, [k2tog, yf, rib 7(8:9:10)] 5 times, k2tog, yf, rib 4(5:4:5).

Work 2 rows in rib.

Cast (bind) off in rib.

TO FINISH

Place markers 10(11:12:13) cm/4(4¼:4¾:5)in down from shoulder seams. Sew sleeves in place between these markers. Join side and sleeve seams. Using C and embroidery thread, embroider details to chart one and chart two. Sew on buttons, matching buttonholes.

Duck Beak Booties

MEASUREMENTS

TO FIT AGES
0–3   3–6 months

SPECIAL ABBREVIATIONS

k1B: Knit 1 st (or number indicated) in yarn B (or other colour indicated).

TENSION

28 sts and 50 rows to 10cm/4in over g st using 2.75mm (US 2) needles.

26 sts and 48 rows to 10cm/4in over g st using 3mm (US 2–3) needles.

MATERIALS

Yarn quantities are based on average requirements and are therefore approximate.

- 50g/1¾oz balls of Debbie Bliss Baby Cashmerino:
  - 1 ball in Baby Blue (A)
  - 1 ball in Acid Yellow (B)
  - 1 ball in Ecru (C)

0–3 MONTHS
- 2 x 2.75mm (US 2) double-pointed needles (DPNs)

3–6 MONTHS
- 2 x 3mm (US 2–3) double-pointed needles (DPNs)

BOTH SIZES
- Stitch holder
- 75cm/29½in narrow ribbon for ties

PATTERN NOTE

A larger needle size is used for the larger booties but instructions remain the same for both sizes.

BOOTIES (MAKE 2)

With 2.75mm (US 2) or 3mm (US 2–3) needles and A, cast on 18 sts (for first half of cuff) and k 16 rows.

Break yarn and leave sts on a holder.

Rep from * to * for second half of cuff.

JOIN CUFF HALVES

Next row: [K1, p1] 9 times across second half of cuff, then [k1, p1] 9 times across first half of cuff.

36 sts.

Next row: [K1, p1] to end.

Rep the last row 6 times more.

SHAPE INSTEP

Next row (right side): K13A, break off A and join B, k10B, turn.

Using B, work as follows.

Next row: K10, turn.

Work 24 rows on centre 10 sts.

Next row: K1, skpo, k4, k2tog, k1.

8 sts.

K 1 row.

Break yarn.

With right side facing and C, returning to sts left at base of instep, pick up and knit 13 sts evenly along side of instep, k across centre 8 sts, then pick up and knit 13 sts evenly along other side of instep, k rem 13 sts.

60 sts.

K 11 rows.

Work 7 rows in st st, beginning with a k row.

Next row: [P next st tog with corresponding st 7 rows below] to end.

Break yarn.

SHAPE SOLE

Next row: Slip first 25 sts onto right hand needle, rejoin B and k10 sts, turn.

Next row: K9, k2tog, turn.

Rep last row until 20 sts rem, then k to end.

Cast (bind) off.

MAKING UP

Join back seam. With back seam to centre of cast (bind) off, join heel seam. Fold 4 rows of instep together at toe and seam to create a small ridge at front of bootie.

TO FINISH

Thread narrow ribbon through the rib, starting and ending either side of the centre stitch. Secure at back of heel. Tie in a bow and trim as necessary.

Squirrel Nutkin™

This tale is about a cheeky and rather lazy squirrel who, along with his brothers and cousins, sail to an island on a boat made of twigs to gather nuts to prepare for winter. Squirrel Nutkin annoys Old Brown, an owl and the owner of the island, by asking him riddles instead of supplying him with gifts in return for gathering nuts. Old Brown captures him, and in Nutkin's struggle to escape he loses his tail. From now on Nutkin will not be asking riddles!

This layette will provide plenty of nuts for Squirrel Nutkin and his family over winter, with acorns featuring in a Fair Isle yoked sweater, a cosy shawl-collared jacket, and a blanket. For extra nibbles, there is also an acorn beanie hat.

Acorn Yoke Sweater

MEASUREMENTS

TO FIT AGES
0-3   3-6   6-9   9-12 months

FINISHED SIZES
Chest
51   56   62   67 cm
20   22   24½   26¼ in

Length to shoulder
27   28   29.5   30 cm
10¾   11   11½   11¾ in

Sleeve length
13   15   17   19 cm
5   6   6¾   7½ in

MATERIALS

Yarn quantities are based on average requirements and are therefore approximate.

- 50g/1¾oz balls of West Yorkshire Spinners Bo Peep DK:
  - 3(3:3:4) balls in Golden Lion (A)
  - 1 ball in Treehouse (B)
  - 1 ball in Safari Park (C)
  - 1 ball in Fluffy Clouds (D)
  - 1 ball in Tin Man (E)
- Pair of 3.25mm (US 3) knitting needles
- Pair of 4mm (US 6) knitting needles
- 4mm (US 6) circular needle, 80cm/32in long
- 3 medium buttons
- Stitch markers
- Stitch holders or spare needles

TENSION

22 sts and 28 rows to 10cm/4in square over st st using 4mm (US 6) needles.

SPECIAL ABBREVIATIONS

wrap 1 on a k side row: yarn to front, slip next st onto right hand needle, yarn to back, slip st back onto left hand needle, when working across the wrapped st on the next row, work the wrapped st and the wrapping loop tog as one st.

wrap 1 on a p side row: yarn to back, slip next st onto right hand needle, yarn to front, slip st back onto left hand needle, when working across the wrapped st on the next row, work the wrapped st and the wrapping loop tog as one st.

CHART NOTES

Read chart from right to left when knitting across chart sts and from left to right when purling across chart sts.

Note that chart one begins on a wrong side row.

If preferred colourwork can be worked using Swiss darning/duplicate stitch on completion.

SWEATER BACK

With 3.25mm (US 3) needles and A, cast on 57(63:69:75) sts.

1st rib row: K1, [p1, k1] to end.

2nd rib row: P1, [k1, p1] to end.

These 2 rows **set** rib.

Work 3 more rows in rib.

Next row: P2tog, p to end.

56(62:68:74) sts.

Change to 4mm (US 6) needles.

Work in st st, beginning with a k row, until back measures 16cm/6¼in from cast-on edge, ending with a p row.

SHAPE ARMHOLES

Cast (bind) off 3 sts at beg of next 2 rows.

50(56:62:68) sts.

Leave these sts on a holder or spare needle.

SWEATER FRONT

Work as for back to 12 rows before shape armholes.

1st row: K22, wrap 1, turn.

2nd row: P to end.

3rd row: K18, wrap 1, turn.

4th row: P to end.

5th row: K14, wrap 1, turn.

6th row: P to end.

7th row: K10, wrap 1, turn.

8th row: P to end.

9th row: K6, wrap 1, turn.

10th row: P to end.

11th row: K to end, working wraps and wrapped sts together.

12th row: P22, wrap 1, turn.

13th row: K to end.

14th row: P18, wrap 1, turn.

15th row: K to end.

16th row: P14, wrap 1, turn.

17th row: K to end.

18th row: P10, wrap 1, turn.

19th row: K to end.

20th row: P6, wrap 1, turn.

21st row: K to end.

22nd row: P to end, working wraps and wrapped sts together.

SHAPE ARMHOLES

Cast (bind) off 3 sts at beg of next 2 rows.

50(56:62:68) sts.

Leave these sts on a holder or spare needle.

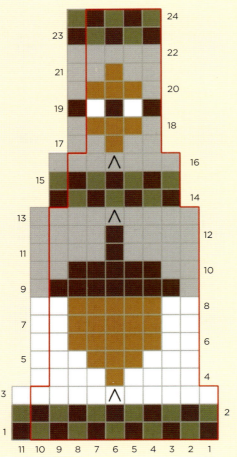

CHART ONE

KEY
- ☐ RS: knit / WS: purl
- ∧ RS: sl1, k2tog, psso / WS: sl1 wyif, p2tog tbl, psso
- ■ A
- ■ B
- ■ C
- ☐ D
- ■ E
- ▭ Pattern repeat

SLEEVES (MAKE 2)

With 3.25mm (US 3) needles and A, cast on 33(35:37:39) sts.

1st row: K1, [p1, k1] to end.

2nd row: P1, [k1, p1] to end.

These 2 rows **set** rib.

Work 3 more rows in rib.

Next row: P to end.

Cont in st st, work 4 rows, beginning with a k row.

Inc row: K3, m1, k to last 3 sts, m1, k3.

Work 3 rows in st st.

Rep the last 4 rows 4(5:6:7) times more.

43(47:51:55) sts.

Cont straight in st st until sleeve measures 13(15:17:19)cm/5(6:6¾:7½)in from cast-on edge, ending with a p row.

Cast (bind) off 3 sts at beg of next 2 rows.

37(41:45:49) sts.

YOKE

With right side facing, using 4mm (US 6) circular needle and A, k across 50(56:62:68) sts for back, 37(41:45:49) sts for first sleeve, 50(56:62:68) sts for front and 37(41:45:49) sts for second sleeve, increasing 1 st on last st. Join to work in the round, place marker for beg of round.

175(195:215:235) sts.

K 3(5:9:11) rounds.

P 1 round.

K 1 round.

DIVIDE FOR BACK NECK OPENING

Next round (partial): K23(26:29:32), cast (bind) off 4 sts, k around to gap at beg of cast off, turn.

171(191:211:231) sts.

PLACE CHART

Working back and forth in rows, cont as follows.

Next row (wrong side): Working from 1st row of chart one, p1 st before patt rep, rep 10-st patt rep 17(19:21:23) times.

Next row (right side): Working from 2nd row of chart one, rep 10-st patt rep 17(19:21:23) times, k1 st after patt rep.

These 2 rows **set** chart placement.

Work 3rd–24th rows of chart one.

69(77:85:93) sts.

Break off B, C, D and E. Cont with A only.

Next row: P2, [p2, p2tog] to last 3 sts, p3.

53(59:65:71) sts.

Change to 3.25mm (US 3) needles.

Work in k1, p1 rib as set on back, beginning with 2nd row, for 5 rows.

Cast (bind) off in rib.

LEFT BACK OPENING EDGE

With right side facing, using 3.25mm (US 3) needles and A, pick up and knit 27 sts evenly up left back opening edge.

K 6 rows.

Cast (bind) off knitwise.

RIGHT BACK OPENING EDGE

With right side facing, using 3.25mm (US 3) needles and A, pick up and knit 27 sts evenly down right back opening edge.

K 3 rows.

Buttonhole row: K3, yf, k2tog, [k8, yf, k2tog] twice, k2.

K 2 rows.

Cast (bind) off knitwise.

MAKING UP

Join side and sleeve seams. Sew right back edge over left back edge to cast-off (bound-off) sts. Sew on buttons, matching buttonholes on back neck opening.

Nutkin Jacket

MEASUREMENTS

TO FIT AGES
0-3 3-6 6-9 9-12 months

FINISHED SIZES
Chest
55   59   62   67 cm
21¾ 23¼ 24½ 26¼ in

Length to shoulder
27   28   29   30 cm
10¾ 11   11½ 11¾ in

Sleeve length
13   15   17   19 cm
5   6   6¾   7½ in

MATERIALS

Yarn quantities are based on average requirements and are therefore approximate.

- 50g/1¾oz balls of West Yorkshire Spinners Bo Peep DK:
  - 1(1:1:1) balls in Golden Lion (A)
  - 1(1:2:2) ball in Treehouse (B)
  - 1(1:1:1) ball in Fluffy Clouds (C)
  - 2(2:2:3) ball in Tin Man (D)
- Pair of 3.25mm (US 3) knitting needles
- Pair of 4mm (US 6) knitting needles
- 4mm (US 6) circular needle, 80cm/32in long
- 3 medium buttons
- Stitch markers
- Stitch holders or spare needles
- Small amount of Black DK yarn for details

TENSION

22 sts and 28 rows to 10cm/4in square over st st using 4mm (US 6) needles.

SPECIAL ABBREVIATIONS

k1A: Knit 1 st (or number indicated) in yarn A (or other colour indicated).

wrap 1 on a k side row: yarn to front, slip next st onto right hand needle, yarn to back, slip st back onto left hand needle, when working across the wrapped st on the next row, work the wrapped st and the wrapping loop tog as one st.

wrap 1 on a p side row: yarn to back, slip next st onto right hand needle, yarn to front, slip st back onto left hand needle, when working across the wrapped st on the next row, work the wrapped st and the wrapping loop tog as one st.

CHART NOTES

Read charts from right to left when knitting across chart sts and from left to right when purling across chart sts.

If preferred colourwork can be worked using Swiss darning/duplicate stitch on completion.

JACKET BODY

Fronts and back are worked in one piece to armhole.

With 3.25mm (US 3) needles and B, cast on 122(130:138:146) sts.

1st rib row: K2, [p2, k2] to end.

2nd rib row: P2, [k2, p2] to end.

These 2 rows **set** rib.

Work 5 more rows in rib.

Next row: P60(64:68:72), p2tog, p60(64:68:72). 121(129:137:145) sts.

Change to 4mm (US 6) needles and D.

Work 2 rows in st st, beginning with a k row.

Change to C.

P 2 rows.

1st row: Working from 1st row of chart one, k1 st before patt rep, [work 8-st patt rep] 15(16:17:18) times.

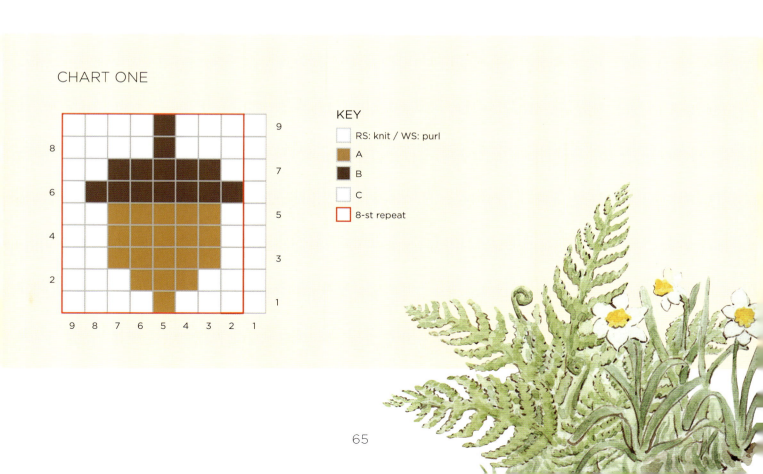

CHART TWO

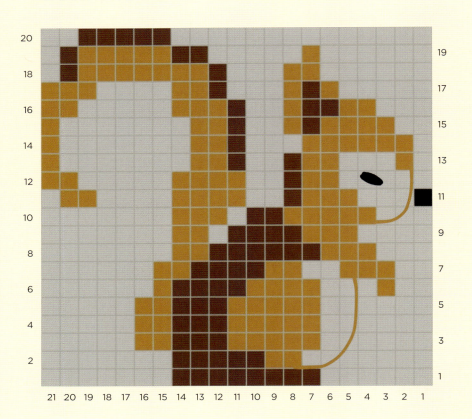

KEY
- ☐ RS: knit / WS: purl
- A
- B
- D
- Black

CHART THREE

KEY
- ☐ RS: knit / WS: purl
- A
- B
- D
- Black

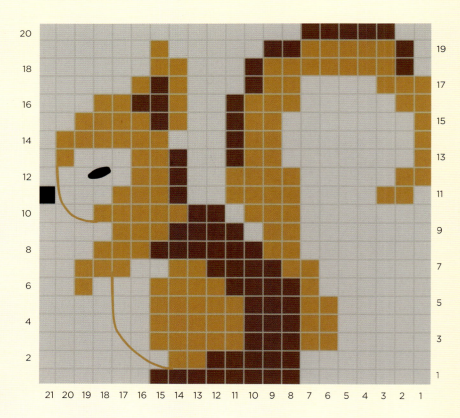

2nd row: Working from 2nd row of chart one, [work 8-st patt rep] 15(16:17:18) times, p1 st after patt rep.

These 2 rows **set** chart placement.

Work 3rd–9th rows of chart one.

Break off A and B. Cont in C only.

P 1 row.

Change to D.

P 2 rows.

1st row: K4(6:6:6)D, work across 21 sts of 1st row of chart two, k8(10:12:16)D, work across 21 sts of 1st row of chart three, k13(13:17:17)D, work across 21 sts of 1st row of chart two, k8(10:12:16)D, work across 21 sts of 1st row of chart three, k4(6:6:6)D.

2nd row: P4(6:6:6)D, work across 21 sts of 2nd row of chart three, p8(10:12:16)D, work across 21 sts of 2nd row of chart two, p13(13:17:17)D, work across 21 sts of 2nd row of chart three, p8(10:12:16)D, work across 21 sts of 2nd row of chart two, p4(6:6:6)D.

These 2 rows **set** chart placements.

Work 3rd–20th rows of charts two and three.

Break off A and B. Cont in D only.

Work 2 rows in st st, beginning with a k row.

DIVIDE FOR RAGLANS

Next row: K25(27:29:31), cast (bind) off 4 sts, place marker, cast off 4 sts, k55(59:63:67) including last st used in casting off, cast off 4 sts, place marker, cast off 4 sts, k rem 25(27:29:31) sts including last st used in casting off.

25(27:29:31) sts for each front; 55(59:63:67) sts for back.

Work each set of sts separately as follows.

LEFT FRONT

Working across first 25(27:29:31) sts, p to end.

SHAPE RAGLAN

Next row: K2, skpo, k to end.

Next row: P to end.

Rep last 2 rows 4 times more.

20(22:24:26) sts.

Place marker at neck edge of last row.

SHAPE SLOPE

Next row: K2, skpo, k to last 4 sts, k2tog, k2.

Next row: P to end.

Rep last 2 rows 6(7:8:9) times more.

6 sts.

Next row: K1, sl1, k2tog, psso, k2.

4 sts.

Next row: P4.

Next row: Sl1, k2tog, psso, k1.

2 sts.

Next row: P2.

Next row: K2tog and fasten off.

BACK

Working across next 55(59:63:67) sts, p to end.

SHAPE RAGLAN

Next row: K2, skpo, k to last 4 sts, k2og, k2.

Next row: P to end.

Rep last 2 rows 14(15:16:17) times more.

25(27:29:31) sts.

Leave rem sts on a holder.

RIGHT FRONT

Working across next 25(27:29:31) sts, p to end.

SHAPE RAGLAN

Next row: K to last 4 sts, k2tog, k2.

Next row: P to end.

Rep last 2 rows 4 times more.

20(22:24:26) sts.

Place marker at neck edge of last row.

SHAPE SLOPE

Next row: K2, skpo, k to last 4 sts, k2tog, k2.

Next row: P to end.

Rep last 2 rows 6(7:8:9) times more.

6 sts.

Next row: K2, sl1, k2tog, psso, k1.

4 sts.

Next row: P to end.

Next row: K1, sl1, k2tog, psso.

2 sts.

Next row: P2.

Next row: K2tog and fasten off.

SLEEVES

With 3.25mm (US 3) needles and B, cast on 46(50:54:58) sts.

1st row: K2, [p2, k2] to end.

2nd row: P2, [k2, p2] to end.

These 2 rows **set** rib.

Work a 5 more rows in rib.

Next row: P2tog, to end.

45(49:53:57) sts.

Change to 4mm (US 6) needles and D.

Work 2 rows in st st, beginning with a k row.

Change to C.

P 2 rows.

Work 2 rows in st st, beginning with a k row.

1st row: Working from 1st row of chart one, k2(1:2:1)C before rep, [work 8-st patt rep] 5(6:6:7) times, k3(0:3:0)C after rep.

2nd row: Working from 2nd row of chart one, p3(0:3:0)C before rep, [work 8-st patt rep] 5(6:6:7) times, p2(1:2:1)C after rep.

These 2 rows **set** chart placement.

Work 3rd–9th rows of chart one.

Break off A and B. Cont in C only.

P 1 row.

Change to D.

P 1 row.

Cont straight in st st, beginning with a p row, until sleeve measures 13(15:17:19) cm/5(6:6¾:7½)in from cast-on edge, ending with a p row.

SHAPE RAGLAN

Cast (bind) off 4 sts at beg of next 2 rows.

37(41:45:49) sts.

Next row: K2, skpo, k to last 4 sts, k2tog, k2.

Next row: P2, p2tog, p to last 4 sts, p2togtbl, p2.

Rep last 2 rows 1(2:3:4) times more.

29 sts.

Next row: K2, skpo, k to last 4 sts, k2tog, k2.

Next row: P to end.

Rep last 2 rows 11 times more.

5 sts.

Leave rem sts on a holder.

MAKING UP

Join raglan seams.

FRONT BANDS

With right side facing, using 3.25mm (US 3) needles and B, beginning at right front edge, pick up and knit 44 sts evenly up to marker, remove marker and place on current st, pick up and knit 14(16:18:20) sts up to sleeve head, k5 sts across first sleeve, k25(27:29:31) sts along back neck and k5 sts across second sleeve, pick up and knit 14(16:18:20) sts evenly down left front to marker, pick up and knit 1 st, remove marker and place on current st, pick up and knit 43 sts down rem left front to cast-on edge.

151(157:163:169) sts.

K 3 rows.

Buttonhole row: K4, [yf, k2tog, k15] twice, yf, k2tog, k to end.

Next row: K to 2nd marker, wrap 1, turn.

Next row: K to marker, wrap 1, turn.

Next 2 rows: K to 4 sts before marker, wrap 1, turn.

Next 2 rows: K to 8 sts before marker, wrap 1, turn.

Next 2 rows: K to 10 sts before marker, wrap 1, turn.

Next 2 rows: K to 12 sts before marker, wrap 1, turn.

Next row: K to end, working wraps and wrapped sts together.

Next row: K to end.

Cast (bind) off.

TO FINISH

Join side and sleeve seams. Using A, work outline embroidery on chart two and chart three. Using Black, work face embroidery on chart two and chart three. Sew on buttons, matching buttonholes.

Owl Island Blanket

MEASUREMENTS

FINISHED SIZE
Length 59cm/23¼in

Width 50cm/19¾in

SPECIAL ABBREVIATIONS

bobble st: K in front, back, front and back of next st, turn, p4, turn, k4, turn, p4, turn, [k2tog] twice, then pass first k2tog over 2nd.

C4B – cable 4 back: Slip 2 sts onto cable needle and hold to back of work, k2, then k2 from cable needle.

C4F – cable 4 front: Slip 2 sts onto cable needle and hold at front of work, k2, then k2 from cable needle.

T3R – cross 3 right: Slip 1 st onto cable needle and hold in back of work, k2, then p1 from cable needle.

T3L – cross 3 left: Slip 2 sts onto cable needle and hold at front of work, p1, then k2 from cable needle.

MATERIALS

Yarn quantities are based on average requirements and are therefore approximate.

- 50g/1¾oz balls of West Yorkshire Spinners Bo Peep DK:
    - 1 ball in Golden Lion (A)
    - 2 balls in Treehouse (B)
    - 2 balls in Safari Park (C)
    - 2 balls in Fluffy Clouds (D)
    - 2 balls in Tin Man (E)
- Pair of 3.25mm (US 3) knitting needles
- Pair of 4mm (US 6) knitting needles
- Cable needle
- Small amount of Black DK yarn for details
- Small amount of toy stuffing (filling)
- Optional 3cm/1¼in pom-pom maker

TENSION

22 sts and 28 rows to 10cm/4in square over st st using 4mm (US 6) needles.

CHART NOTES

Read charts from right to left when working right side rows and left to right when working wrong side rows.

If preferred colourwork can be worked using Swiss darning/ duplicate stitch on completion.

SQUIRREL SQUARE ONE (MAKE 2)

With 4mm (US 6) needles and E, cast on 29 sts.

K 3 rows.

Work square from chart one.

K 2 rows.

Cast (bind) off knitwise.

Using A, work outline embroidery on chart one. Using Black, work face embroidery on chart one. With C and using photographs as guidance, embroider grass blades randomly beneath the squirrel.

SQUIRREL SQUARE TWO (MAKE 2)

With 4mm (US 6) needles and D, cast on 29 sts.

K 3 rows.

Work square from chart two.

K 2 rows.

Cast (bind) off knitwise.

Using A, work outline embroidery on chart two. Using Black, work face embroidery on chart two. With C and using photographs as guidance, embroider grass blades randomly beneath the squirrel.

MUSHROOM SQUARE ONE (MAKE 2)

With 4mm (US 6) needles and C, cast on 29 sts.

K 3 rows.

Work square from chart three.

K 2 rows.

Cast (bind) off knitwise.

MUSHROOM SQUARE TWO (MAKE 2)

With 4mm (US 6) needles and B, cast on 29 sts.

K 3 rows.

Work square from chart four.

K 2 rows.

Cast (bind) off knitwise.

ACORNS AND LEAVES SQUARE ONE (MAKE 2)

With 4mm (US 6) needles and D, cast on 29 sts.

K 3 rows.

Work square from chart five.

K 2 rows.

Cast (bind) off knitwise.

ACORNS AND LEAVES SQUARE TWO (MAKE 2)

With 4mm (US 6) needles and D, cast on 29 sts.

K 3 rows.

Work square from chart six.

K 2 rows.

Cast (bind) off knitwise.

CHART ONE

KEY

□	RS: knit / WS: purl
•	RS: purl / WS: knit
■ (tan)	A
■ (brown)	B
■ (grey)	E
■	Black

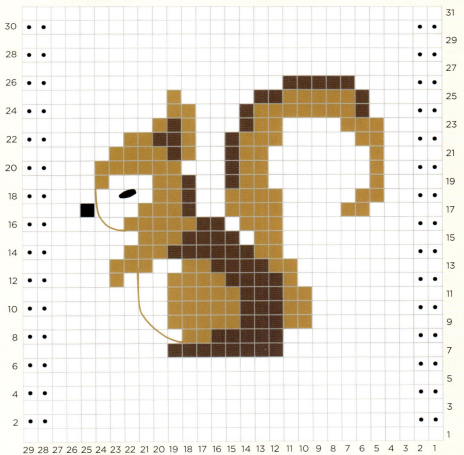

CHART TWO

KEY

□	RS: knit / WS: purl
•	RS: purl / WS: knit
■ (tan)	A
■ (brown)	B
□	D
■	Black

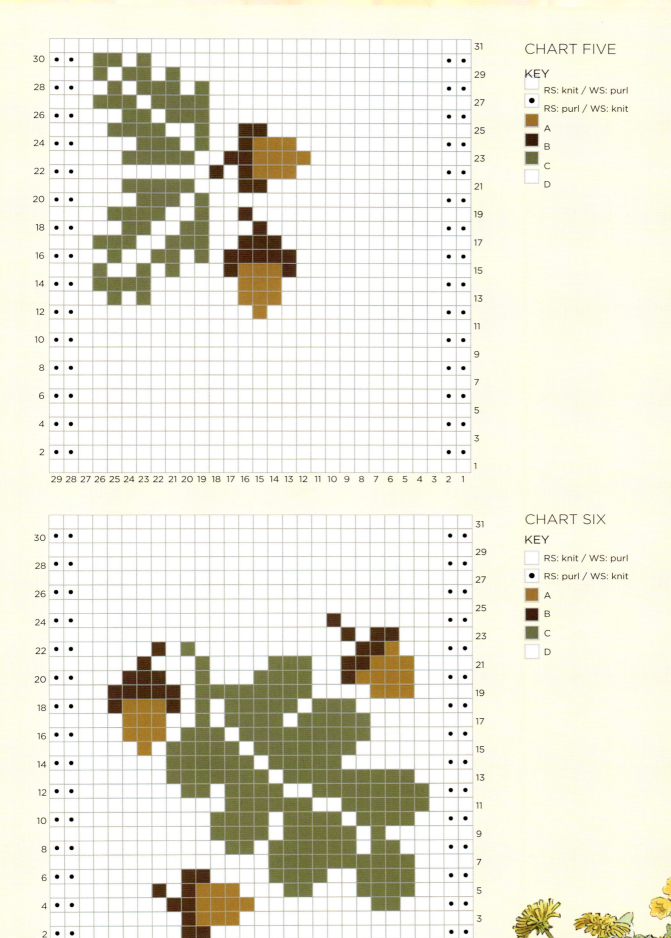

CHART SEVEN

KEY
- ☐ RS: knit / WS: purl
- • RS: purl / WS: knit
- ■ A
- ■ B
- ■ C
- ☐ D
- ■ E

CHART EIGHT

KEY
- ☐ RS: knit / WS: purl
- • RS: purl / WS: knit
- ⧗ C4B
- ⧖ C4F
- ⟋ T3R
- ⟍ T3L
- ⓫ bobble st

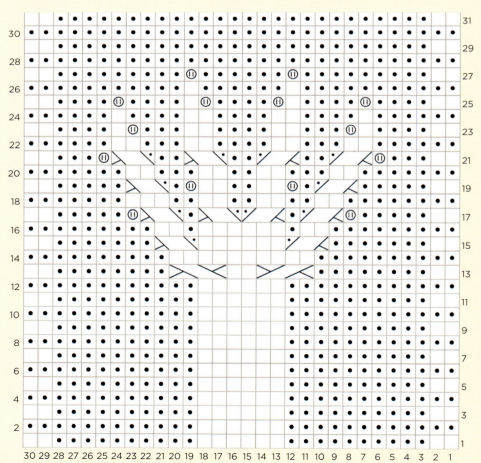

FAIR ISLE SQUARE (MAKE 4)

With 4mm (US 6) needles and A, cast on 29 sts.

K 3 rows.

Work square from chart seven.

K 2 rows.

Cast (bind) off knitwise.

CABLE TREE SQUARE ONE (MAKE 2)

With 4mm (US 6) needles and B, cast on 29 sts.

K 2 rows.

Next row: K24, kfb, k24.

30 sts.

Work square from chart eight.

Next row: K24, k2tog, k24.

29 sts.

K 1 row.

Cast (bind) off knitwise.

CABLE TREE SQUARE TWO (MAKE 2)

With 4mm (US 6) needles and C, cast on 29 sts.

K 2 rows.

Next row: K24, kfb, k24.

30 sts.

Work square from chart eight.

Next row: K24, k2tog, k24.

29 sts.

K 1 row.

Cast (bind) off knitwise.

ACORNS (MAKE 2)

With 3.25mm (US 3) needles and B, cast on 5 sts.

1st row (right side): [Kfb] 5 times.

10 sts.

2nd row: K to end.

3rd row: [Kfb] 10 times.

20 sts.

4th row: K to end.

5th row: [K2tog] 10 times.

10 sts.

6th row: K to end.

Change to A.

Work 5 rows in st st, beginning with a k row.

12th row: [P2tog] 5 times.

5 sts.

13th row: Skpo, k1, k2tog.

3 sts.

Break yarn and thread through rem 3 sts, pull up tight.

Join seam along yarn A edges. Insert stuffing, cont to join seam along yarn B edges, stuffing as you go. Make sure the top of the acorn is closed, leaving a length of yarn to sew to blanket.

LEAVES (MAKE 2)

With 4mm (US 6) needles and C, cast on 17 sts.

Work 4 rows in st st, beginning with a k row.

Next row: K1, [yf, k2tog] 3 times, k3, [yf, k2tog] 3 times, k1.

Work 4 rows in st st, beginning with a p row.

Work cast (bind) off as follows:

With right hand needle, pick up first st on cast-on row, place it on left hand needle and k2tog with first st on left hand needle, pick up and place next st from cast-on edge onto left hand needle and k2tog with next st on needle, take first st on right hand needle over second to cast (bind) off. Casting (binding) off sts in this way, cont to k each st together with corresponding st on cast-on edge and cast (bind) off all sts.

Fold in half and sew straight edges together.

MAKING UP

Join blanket squares together using photo for placement. Sew a leaf and acorn to bottom left corner and top right corner.

Acorn Hat

MEASUREMENTS

TO FIT AGES
0-3   3-6   6-12 months

MATERIALS

Yarn quantities are based on average requirements and are therefore approximate.

- 50g/1¾oz balls of West Yorkshire Spinners Bo Peep DK:
  - 1(2:2) balls in Golden Lion (A)
  - 1 ball in Treehouse (B)
  - 1 ball in Safari Park (C)
- 4mm (US 6) circular needle, 30cm/12in long
- A set of 4mm (US 6) double-pointed needles (DPNs)
- Stitch marker

TENSION

22 sts and 28 rounds to 10cm/4in square over st st using 4mm (US 6) needles.

HAT

With 4mm (US 6) circular needle and B, cast on 75(83:91) sts.

Join to work in the round, being careful not to twist stitches, place marker for beg of round.

Work 14 rounds in st st (k every round).

Break off B.

Join A.

Cont in st st until hat measures 11(13:15)cm/4¼(5:6)in from cast-on edge.

SHAPE CROWN

Change to 4mm (US 6) DPNs when stitch count becomes too small for your circular needle.

1st round: K9(10:11), [s2kpo, k15(17:19)] 3 times, s2kpo, k9(10:11).

67(75:83) sts.

Work 1 round in st st.

3rd round: K8(9:10), [s2kpo, k13(15:17)] 3 times, s2kpo, k8(9:10).

59(67:75) sts.

Work 1 round in st st.

5th round: K7(8:9), [s2kpo, k11(13:15)] 3 times, s2kpo, k7(8:9).

51(59:67) sts.

Work 1 round in st st.

7th round: K6(7:8), [s2kpo, k9(11:13)] 3 times, s2kpo, k6(7:8).

43(51:59) sts.

Work 1 round in st st.

9th round: K5(6:7), [s2kpo, k7(9:11)] 3 times, s2kpo, k5(6:7).

35(43:51) sts.

Work 1 round in st st.

11th round: K4(5:6), [s2kpo, k5(7:9)] 3 times, s2kpo, k4(5:6).

27(35:43) sts.

Work 1 round in st st.

2ND AND 3RD SIZES ONLY

13th round: K-(4:5), [s2kpo, k-(5:7)] 3 times, s2kpo, k-(4:5).

-(27:35) sts.

Work 1 round in st st.

3RD SIZE ONLY

15th round: K-(-:4), [s2kpo, k-(-:5)] 3 times, s2kpo, k-(-:4).

-(-:27) sts.

Work 1 round in st st.

ALL SIZES

Next round: K1, k2tog, [s2kpo] to last 3 sts, skpo, k1.

11 sts.

Next round: K2, [k2tog] 4 times, k1.

7 sts.

Leaving a long end, break yarn and thread through rem sts, pull up and secure.

LEAVES (MAKE 2)

With 4mm (US 6) needles and C, cast on 17 sts.

Work 4 rows in st st, beginning with a k row.

Next row: K1, [yf, k2tog] 3 times, k3, [yf, k2tog] 3 times, k1.

Work 4 rows in st st, beginning with a p row.

Work cast (bind) off as follows:

With right hand needle, pick up first st on cast-on row, place it on left hand needle and k2tog with first st on left hand needle, pick up and place next st from cast-on edge onto left hand needle and k2tog with next st on needle, take first st on right hand needle over second to cast (bind) off. Casting (binding) off sts in this way, cont to k each st together with corresponding st on cast-on edge and cast (bind) off all sts.

Fold in half and sew straight edges together.

STEM

With 4mm (US 6) DPNs and B, cast on 6 sts.

I-cord row: K6, do not turn, slip sts to other end of needle.

This row **sets** i-cord.

Cont in this way, making sure to pull work tightly at beginning of each row, until stem measures 2.5cm/1in from cast-on edge.

Final row: [K2tog] 3 times.

3 sts.

Break yarn leaving a long end and thread through rem 3 sts.

TO FINISH

Using photo as a guide to placement, attach the stem and the leaves to the top of the hat.

Mrs. Tiggy-Winkle™

Mrs. Tiggy-Winkle is a fastidious laundress for the forest animals. Meeting Mrs. Tiggy-Winkle while searching for lost handkerchiefs, Lucie has tea, finds her missing items and manages to avoid the prickles peeping out of Mrs. Tiggy-Winkle's dress! When Lucie says goodbye, she sees only a small hedgehog and no clothes at all. Was it a dream?

The gingham in this layette reflects Mrs. Tiggy-Winkle's dress in the beautiful watercolour wash of Beatrix Potter's illustrations. Small hedgehogs scamper around Mrs. Tiggy-Winkle at the centre of the blanket. A crossover (wrap) cardigan, strappy shoes and hedgehog rattle complete the set.

Mrs. Tiggy-Winkle™ Blanket

MEASUREMENTS

FINISHED SIZE
Length 58cm/22¾in

Width 58cm/22¾in

MATERIALS

Yarn quantities are based on average requirements and are therefore approximate.

- 50g/1¾oz balls of Debbie Bliss Eco Baby Wool:
  - 3 balls in Ecru (A)
  - 3 balls in Rose (B)
  - 1 ball in Bark (C)
- 50g/1¾oz balls of Debbie Bliss Baby Cashmerino:
  - 1 ball in Mink (D)
  - Small amount of Black
- Pair of 3mm (US 2-3) knitting needles
- Pair of 3.25mm (US 3) knitting needles

TENSION

25 sts and 34 rows to 10cm/4in square over st st using 3.25mm (US 3) needles.

SPECIAL ABBREVIATIONS

k1A: Knit 1 st (or number indicated) in yarn A (or other colour indicated).

CHART NOTES

Read charts from right to left when knitting across chart sts and from left to right when purling across chart sts.

If preferred colourwork can be worked using Swiss darning/duplicate stitch on completion.

BLANKET

With 3.25mm (US 3) needles and A, cast on 117 sts.

Work 2 rows in st st, beginning with a k row.

LOWER BORDER
**

1st row: K1A, working from 1st row of chart one, k11 sts before rep, [work 26-st rep] 4 times, k1A.

2nd row: P1A, working from 2nd row of chart one, [work 26-st rep] 4 times, p11 sts after rep, p1A.

These 2 rows **set** chart one.

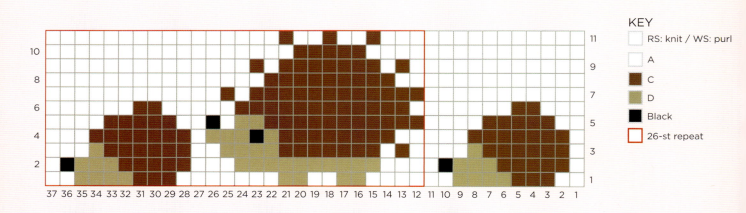

CHART ONE

Work 3rd–11th rows of chart one.

Using A only, work 3 rows in st st, beginning with a p row.

GINGHAM PATT

***

1st row: Working from 1st row of chart two, [work 6-st rep] to last 3 sts, work 3 sts after rep.

2nd row: Working from 2nd row of chart two, work 3 sts before rep, [work 6-st rep] to end.

These 2 rows **set** chart two.

Work a further 50 rows in patt, ending with 4th row of chart two.

****

CENTRAL MOTIF

1st row: Working from 5th row of chart two, [work 6-st rep] 6 times, work 3 sts after rep, work 1st row of chart three, working from 5th row of chart two, [work 6-st rep] 6 times, work 3 sts after rep.

2nd row: Working from 6th row of chart two, work 3 sts before rep, [work 6-st rep] 6 times, work 2nd row of chart three, working from 6th row of chart two, work 3 sts before rep, [work 6-st rep] 6 times.

These 2 rows **set** charts two and three placement.

Work a further 58 rows in patt, completing chart three and ending after 8th row of chart two.

GINGHAM PATT

Rep from *** to **** working chart two only.

UPPER BORDER

Rep from ** to *** for Upper Border working chart one only, and working only 1 row in st st after finishing chart.

With A, cast (bind) off.

RIGHT SIDE EDGING

With right side facing, using 3.25mm (US 3) needles and A, pick up and knit 143 sts evenly up right side edge of blanket.

P 1 row.

1st row: K1A, working from 1st row of chart one, k11 sts before rep, [work 26-st rep] 5 times, k1A.

2nd row: P1A, working from 2nd row of chart one, [work 26-st rep] 5 times, p11 sts after rep, p1A.

These 2 rows **set** chart one.

Work 3rd–11th rows of chart one.

Using A only, work 3 rows in st st, beginning with a p row.

Change to 3mm (US 2–3) needles and B.

K 5 rows.

Cast (bind) off knitwise.

CHART TWO

KEY

- RS: knit / WS: purl
- A
- B
- 6-st repeat

CHART THREE

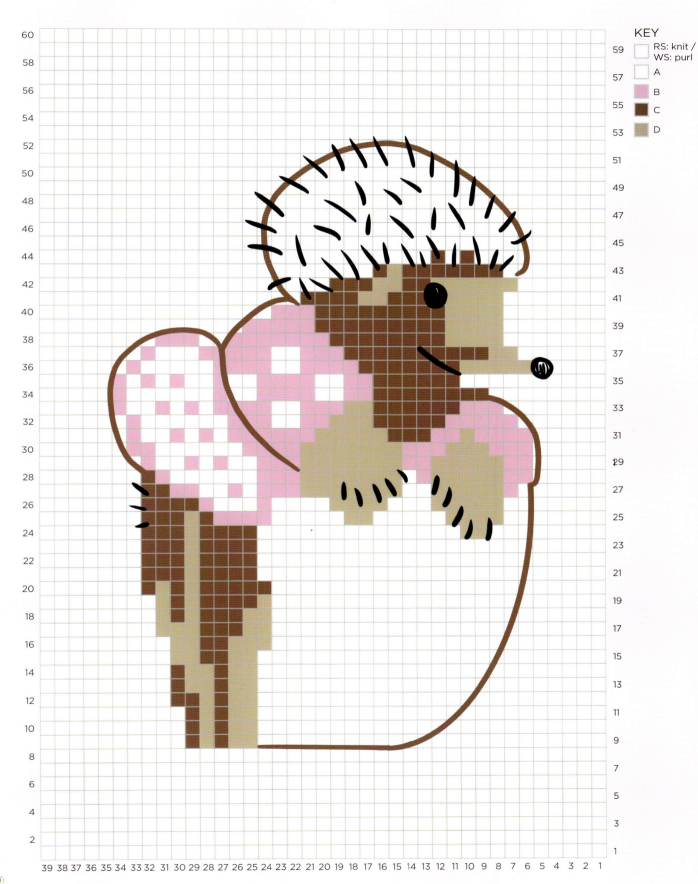

LEFT SIDE EDGING

With right side facing, using 3.25mm (US 3) needles and A, pick up and knit 143 sts evenly down left side edge of blanket.

P 1 row.

1st row: K1A, working from 11th row of chart one, k11 sts before rep, [work 26-st rep] 5 times, k1A.

2nd row: P1A, working from 10th row of chart one, [work 26-st rep] 5 times, p11 sts after rep, p1A.

These 2 rows **set** chart one, working from top to bottom in descending order.

Work 9th–1st rows of chart one.

Using A only, work 3 rows in st st, beginning with a p row.

Change to 3mm (US 2–3) needles and B.

K 5 rows.

Cast (bind) off knitwise.

LOWER EDGE BORDER

With right side facing, using 3mm (US 2–3) needles and B, pick up and knit 141 sts evenly along left side edging, along cast-on row and along right side edging.

K 4 rows.

Cast (bind) off knitwise.

UPPER EDGE BORDER

With right side facing, using 3mm (US 2–3) needles and B, pick up and knit 141 sts evenly along right side edging, along cast-on row and along left side edging.

K 4 rows.

Cast (bind) off knitwise.

TO FINISH

With Black, work face embroidery on chart one and face, spine and claw embroidery on chart three. With D, work outline and detail embroidery on chart three.

Gingham Cardigan

MEASUREMENTS

TO FIT AGES
0-3   3-6   6-9   9-12 months

FINISHED SIZES
Chest
52   58   64   66 cm
20½   22¾   25¼   26 in
Length to shoulder
22   24   26   27 cm
8¾   9½   10¼   10¾ in
Sleeve length
13   15   17   19 cm
5   6   6¾   7½ in

TENSION

25 sts and 34 rows to 10cm/4in square over st st using 3.25mm (US 3) needles.

SPECIAL ABBREVIATIONS

k1A: Knit 1 st (or number indicated) in yarn A (or other colour indicated).

CHART NOTES

Read chart from right to left when knitting across chart sts and from left to right when purling across chart sts.

If preferred colourwork can be worked using Swiss darning/duplicate stitch on completion.

MATERIALS

Yarn quantities are based on average requirements and are therefore approximate.

- 50g/1¾oz balls of Debbie Bliss Eco Baby Wool:
  - 2(3:3:4) balls in Ecru (A)
  - 2(3:3:3) balls in Rose (B)
  - 1(1:1:1) ball in Bark (C)
- 50g/1¾oz balls of Debbie Bliss Baby Cashmerino:
  - 1 ball in Mink (D)
  - Small amount of Black
- Pair of 2.75mm (US 2) knitting needles
- Pair of 3mm (US 2-3) knitting needles
- Pair of 3.25mm (US 3) knitting needles
- Stitch markers
- Stitch holder

CHART FOUR

KEY
- ☐ RS: knit / WS: purl
- ☐ A
- ▩ C
- ▩ D
- ■ Black

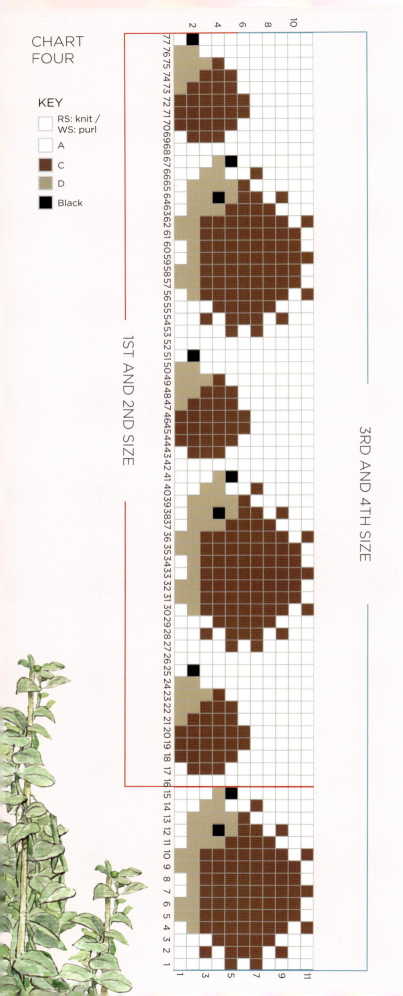

1ST AND 2ND SIZE

3RD AND 4TH SIZE

CARDIGAN BACK

With 2.75mm (US 2) needles and B, cast on 66(72:81:84) sts.

K 3 rows.

Change to 3.25mm (US 3) needles and A.

Work 3 rows in st st, beginning with a p row.

1st row: K2(5:2:4)A, k across 62(62:77:77) sts from 1st row of chart four for your size, k2(5:2:3)A.

2nd row: P2(5:2:3)A, p across 62(62:77:77) sts from 2nd row of chart four, p2(5:2:4)A.

These 2 rows **set** chart.

Work 3rd–11th rows of chart four.

Break off B and D and cont with A only.

P 1 row.

1st row: Working from 1st row of chart two, [work 6-st patt rep] 11(12:13:14) times, work 0(0:3:0) sts after rep.

2nd row: Working from 2nd row of chart two, work 0(0:3:0) sts before rep, rep [6-st patt rep] 11(12:13:14) times.

These 2 rows **set** chart. Cont in chart two patt throughout.

Work 22(24:28:28) rows straight in patt.

SHAPE ARMHOLES

Cast (bind) off 4 sts at beg of next 2 rows.

58(64:73:76) sts.

Work a further 32(36:40:44) rows straight in patt.

SHAPE SHOULDERS

Cast (bind) off 15(17:20:21) sts at beg of next 2 rows.

28(30:33:34) sts.

Slip rem sts onto a holder.

LEFT FRONT

With 2.75mm (US 2) needles and B, cast on 63(69:78:81) sts.

K 3 rows.

Change to 3.25mm (US 3) needles and A.

Work 3 rows in st st, beginning with a p row.

1st row: K0(4:0:2)A, k across 62(62:77:77) sts from 1st row of chart four for your size, k1(3:1:2)A.

2nd row: P1(3:1:2)A, p across 62(62:77:77) sts from 2nd row of chart four for your size, p0(4:0:2)A.

These 2 rows **set** chart.

Work 3rd–11th rows of chart four.

Break off B and D and cont with A only.

P 1 row.

1st row: Working from 1st row of chart two, [work 6-st patt rep] 10(11:13:13) times, work 3(3:0:3) sts after rep.

2nd row: Working from 2nd row of chart two, work 3(3:0:3) sts before rep, [work 6-st patt rep] 10(11:12:13) times.

These 2 rows **set** chart. Cont in chart two patt throughout.

Work 2 rows straight in patt.

Next row: Patt to last 2 sts, k2tog.

Next row: P2tog, patt to end.

Rep the last 2 rows 9(10:12:12) times more.

43(47:52:55) sts.

SHAPE ARMHOLE

Next row: Cast (bind) off 4 sts, patt to last 2 sts, k2tog.

38(42:47:50) sts.

Next row: P2tog, patt to end.

37(41:46:49) sts.

Next row: Patt to last 2 sts, k2tog.

Next row: P2tog, patt to end.

Rep the last 2 rows 10(11:12:13) times more.

15(17:20:21) sts.

Work 10(12:14:16) rows straight in patt, ending with a p row.

SHAPE SHOULDER

Cast (bind) off rem 15(17:20:21) sts.

RIGHT FRONT

With 2.75mm (US 2) needles and B, cast on 63(69:78:81) sts.

K 3 rows.

Change to 3.25mm (US 3) needles and A.

Work 3 rows in st st, beginning with a p row.

1st row: K0(4:0:2)A, k across 62(62:77:77) sts from 1st row of chart four, k1(3:1:2)A.

2nd row: P1(3:1:2) A, p across 62(62:77:77) sts from 2nd row of chart four, p0(4:0:2)A.

These 2 rows **set** chart.

Work 3rd–11th rows of chart four.

Break off B and D and cont with A only.

P 1 row.

1st row: Working from 1st row of chart two, [work 6-st patt rep] 10(11:13:13) times, work 3(3:0:3) sts after rep.

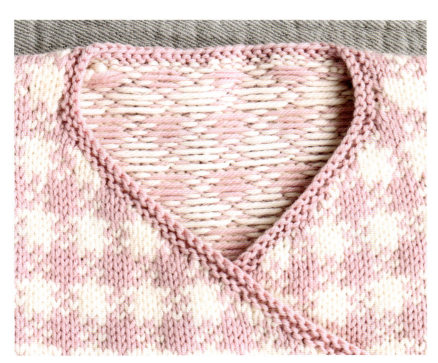

2nd row: Working from 2nd row of chart two, work 3(3:0:3) sts before rep, [work 6-st patt rep] 10(11:12:13) times.

These 2 rows **set** chart. Cont in chart two patt throughout.

Work 2 rows straight in patt.

Next row: Skpo, patt to end.

Next row: Patt to last 2 sts, p2tog.

Rep the last 2 rows 9(10:12:12) times more.

43(47:52:55) sts.

SHAPE ARMHOLE

Next row: Skpo, patt to end.

Next row: Cast (bind) off 4 sts, patt to last 2 sts, p2tog.

37(41:46:49) sts.

Next row: Skpo, patt to end.

Next row: Patt to last 2 sts, p2tog.

Rep the last 2 rows 10(11:12:13) times more.

15(17:20:21) sts.

Work 10(12:14:16) rows straight in patt, ending with a p row.

SHAPE SHOULDER

Cast (bind) off rem 15(17:20:21) sts.

SLEEVES (MAKE 2)

With 2.75mm (US 2) needles and B, cast on 48(54:60:66) sts.

K 3 rows.

Change to 3.25mm (US 3) needles.

1st row: Working from 1st row of chart two, [work 6-st patt rep] 8(9:10:11) times.

2nd row: Working from 2nd row of chart two, [work 6-st patt rep] 8(9:10:11) times.

These 2 rows **set** chart. Cont in chart two patt throughout.

Cont straight until sleeve measures 13(15:17:19) cm/5(6:6¾:7½)in from cast-on edge, ending with a p row.

Place markers at each end of last row.

Work a further 6 rows in patt.

Cast (bind) off.

MAKING UP

Join shoulder seams.

FRONT BANDS

With right side facing, using 3mm (US 2–3) needles and B, beginning at right front edge, pick up and knit 65(69:77:81) sts evenly up to shoulder seam, k across 28(30:33:34) sts left on holder for back neck, pick up and knit 65(69:77:81) sts evenly down to left front cast-on edge.

158(168:187:196) sts.

K 2 rows.

Cast (bind) off knitwise.

TIES (MAKE 2)

With 2.75mm (US 2) needles and B, cast on 5 sts.

Work in g st for 32(36:40:44) cm/12½(14¼:15¾:17¼)in.

Cast (bind) off knitwise.

TO FINISH

With centre of sleeve head to shoulder seam, sew sleeves into armholes between cast-off (bound-off) sts. Join sleeve seams to markers, sew last 6 rows to cast-off sts at armhole. Leaving a small opening in right side seam level with beg of neck shaping, join side seams.

Sew ties to fronts at beg of neck shaping.

Hedgehog Shoes

MEASUREMENTS

TO FIT AGES
0–3   3–6 months

PATTERN NOTE

A larger needle size is used for the larger shoes but instructions remain the same for both sizes.

CHART NOTES

Read charts from right to left when knitting across chart sts and from left to right when purling across chart sts.

Note that charts one and two begin on a wrong side row.

If preferred colourwork can be worked using Swiss darning/duplicate stitch on completion.

TENSION

28 sts and 50 rows to 10cm/4in over g st using 2.75mm (US 2) needles.

29 sts and 38 rows to 10cm/4in over st st using 2.75mm (US 2) needles.

26 sts and 48 rows to 10cm/4in over g st using 3mm (US 2-3) needles.

27 sts and 36 rows to 10cm/4in over st st using 3mm (US 2-3) needles.

SPECIAL ABBREVIATIONS

k1A: Knit 1 st (or number indicated) in yarn A (or other colour indicated).

MATERIALS

Yarn quantities are based on average requirements and are therefore approximate.

- 50g/1¾oz balls of Debbie Bliss Eco Baby Wool:
    - 1 ball in Ecru (A)
    - 1 ball in Rose (B)
    - Small amount of Bark (C)
- 50g/1¾oz balls of Debbie Bliss Baby Cashmerino:
    - Small amount of Mink (D)
    - Small amount of Black

0-3 MONTHS
- Pair of 2.75mm (US 2) knitting needles

3-6 MONTHS
- Pair of 3mm (US 2-3) knitting needles

BOTH SIZES
- 2 small buttons
- Stitch holder

RIGHT SHOE

With 2.75mm (US 2) or 3mm (US 2-3) needles and B, cast on 34 sts.

K 1 row.

1st row: K1, yf, k15, [yf, k1] twice, yf, k15, yf, k1.

39 sts.

2nd row: K to end, working k1tbl into yf of previous row.

3rd row: K2, yf, k15, yf, k2, yf, k3, yf, k15, yf, k2.

44 sts.

4th row: K to end, working k1tbl into yf of previous row.

5th row: K3, yf, k15, [yf, k4] twice, yf, k15, yf, k3.

49 sts.

6th row: K to end, working k1tbl into yf of previous row.

7th row: K4, yf, k15, yf, k5, yf, k6, yf, k15, yf, k4.

54 sts.

8th row: K to end, working k1tbl into yf of previous row.

9th row: K5, yf, k15, [yf, k7] twice, yf, k15, yf, k5.

59 sts.

10th row: K to end, working k1tbl into yf of previous row.

11th row: K7, yf, [k9, yf] 5 times, k7.

65 sts.

12th row: K to end, working k1tbl into yf of previous row.

K 12 rows.

SHAPE INSTEP

1st row: K38, skpo, turn.

Change to A.

2nd row: Sl1, p11, p2tog, turn.

3rd row: Sl1, k11, skpo, turn.

4th row: Sl1, p11, p2tog, turn.

5th row: Sl1, k11, skpo, turn.

SET CHART

6th row: Sl1, p1A, work 1st row of chart one, p1A, p2togA.

7th row: Sl1, k1A, work 2nd row of chart one, k1A, skpoA, turn.

Rep the last 2 rows twice more, working 3rd-6th rows of chart one.

Cont in A only.

12th row: Sl1, p11, p2tog, turn.

13th row: Sl1, k11, skpo, turn.

14th row: Sl1, p11, p2tog, turn.

51 sts.

Change to B.

15th row: Sl1, k to end.

16th row: K to end.

17th row: K to end.

Cast (bind) off knitwise, dec 1 st at each corner.

MAKING UP

Join sole and back seam.

STRAP

With 2.75mm (US 2) needles and B, with right side facing and beginning and ending within 8 sts of back seam, pick up and knit 17 sts along heel.

17 sts.

K 1 row.

**

Next row: Cast on 3 sts, k to end, turn and cast on 19 sts.

39 sts.

K 2 rows.

Buttonhole row: K2, yf, k2tog, k to end.

K 3 rows.

Cast (bind) off.

LEFT SHOE

Work as given for Right Shoe to ** using chart two instead of chart one.

17 sts.

Next row: Cast on 19 sts, k to end, turn and cast on 3 sts.

39 sts.

K 2 rows.

Buttonhole row: K35, yf, k2tog, k2.

K 3 rows.

Cast (bind) off.

TO FINISH

Sew on buttons, matching buttonholes.

CHART ONE

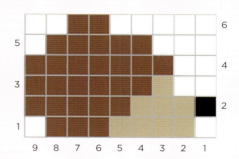

KEY

- RS: knit / WS: purl
- A
- C
- D
- Black

CHART TWO

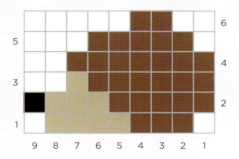

KEY

- RS: knit / WS: purl
- A
- C
- D
- Black

Hedgehog Rattle

MEASUREMENTS

FINISHED SIZE
Length Approx 16cm/6¼in

TENSION

26 sts and 40 rows to 10cm/4in square over st st using 3mm (US 2-3) needles.

MATERIALS

Yarn quantities are based on average requirements and are therefore approximate.

- 50g/1¾oz balls of Debbie Bliss Eco Baby Wool:
  - 1 ball in Bark (A)
- 50g/1¾oz balls of Debbie Bliss Baby Cashmerino:
  - 1 ball in Mink (B)
  - Small amount of Black
- Pair of 3mm (US 2-3) knitting needles
- 1 or 2 jingle bells for rattle
- Washable toy stuffing (filling)

RATTLE

With 3mm (US 2-3) needles and A, cast on 9 sts.

SHAPE BODY

1st row: K1, [kfb] to end.

17 sts.

2nd row: K1, [p1, k1] to end.

3rd row: K1, [kfb] to end.

33 sts.

4th row: K1, [p1, k1] to end.

5th row: K to end.

6th row: K1, [p1, k1] to end.

7th row: K1, [kfb, k1] to end.

49 sts.

8th row: K1, [p1, k1] to end.

9th row: K to end.

10th row: K1, [p1, k1] to end.

11th row: K1, [kfb, k2] to end.

65 sts.

SET PATT

12th row: K1, [p1, k1] to end.

13th row: K to end.

These 2 rows **set** patt.

Work a further 29 rows straight in patt.

43rd row: K1, [k2tog, k1] to end.

49 sts.

44th row: K to end.

SHAPE HEAD

Change to B.

45th row: K to end.

46th row and all wrong side rows: P to end.

47th row: K8, skpo, k6, k2tog, k14, skpo, k6, k2tog, k7.

45 sts.

49th row: K8, skpo, k4, k2tog, k14, skpo, k4, k2tog, k7.

41 sts.

51st row: K8, skpo, k2, k2tog, k14, skpo, k2, k2tog, k7.

37 sts.

53rd row: K8, skpo, k2tog, k14, skpo, k2tog, k7.

33 sts.

55th row: K6, [k2tog] twice, skpo, k10, [k2tog] twice, skpo, k5.

27 sts.

57th row: K5, k2tog, k1, skpo, k8, k2tog, k1, skpo, k4.

23 sts.

59th row: K4, k2tog, k1, skpo, k6, k2tog, k1, skpo, k3.

19 sts.

61st row: K3, k2tog, k1, skpo, k4, k2tog, k1, skpo, k2.

15 sts.

63rd row: K2, k2tog, k1, skpo, k2, k2tog, k1, skpo, k1.

11 sts.

65th row: K1, [k2tog] to end.

6 sts.

Leaving a long end, break yarn and thread through rem sts, pull up and secure.

NOSE

With 3mm (US2–3) needles and Black, cast on 2 sts.

1st row: [Kfb] twice.

4 sts.

2nd row: P to end.

3rd row: K to end.

4th row: P to end.

5th row: [K2tog] twice.

2 sts.

Leaving a long end, break yarn and thread through rem sts, pull up and secure.

MAKING UP

Join side seam of rattle, stuffing as you go and adding jingle bells in centre of stuffing. Attach nose securely to fasten-off point after 65th row. Using Black, embroider eyes to either side of face approximately 6 stitches apart and 3 rows in length, beginning after 48th row.

Tom Kitten™

The Tale of Tom Kitten introduces Tom Kitten and his sisters Mittens and Moppet. When their mother Tabitha Twitchit invites friends for tea she wants them in clean, neat clothes, though the kittens find them uncomfortable. Unwisely Tabitha sends the kittens out to play before the party. After various mishaps, the mischievous kittens get their clothes dirty, and then lose them completely!

The top and trousers are based on what Tom Kitten wore, but unlike his, this set is not uncomfortable as the beautifully soft yarn is gentle against a baby's skin. This layette features simple stitches and styles. It includes a cuddle-into, hooded cat blanket in garter stitch and a cute kitten cap too.

Kitten Cardigan

MEASUREMENTS

TO FIT AGES
0–3   3–6   6–9   9–12 months

FINISHED SIZES
Chest
51   55   60   64 cm
20   21¾   23¾   25¼ in

Length to shoulder
19   20   21   22 cm
7½   7¾   8¼   8¾ in

Sleeve length
13   15   17   19 cm
5   6   6¾   7½ in

MATERIALS

Yarn quantities are based on average requirements and are therefore approximate.

- 50g/1¾oz balls of West Yorkshire Spinners Pure DK:
  - 2(2:3:3) balls in River
- Pair of 3.25mm (US 3) knitting needles
- Pair of 4mm (US 6) knitting needles
- 2 medium buttons
- Stitch holders or spare needles
- Stitch markers

TENSION

22 sts and 28 rows to 10cm/4in square over st st using 4mm (US 6) needles.

CARDIGAN BACK

With 3.25mm (US 3) needles, cast on 56(60:66:70) sts.

K 7 rows.

Change to 4mm (US 6) needles.

Cont in st st, beginning with a k row, until back measures 8cm/3¼in from cast-on edge, ending with a p row.

SHAPE ARMHOLES

Cast (bind) off 4 sts at beg of next 2 rows.

48(52:58:62) sts.

Cont in st st, beginning with a k row, until armholes measure 10(11:12:13)cm/4(4¼:4¾:5) in from cast-off (bound-off) edge, ending with a p row.

SHAPE SHOULDERS

Cast (bind) off 14(15:17:18) sts at beg of next 2 rows.

20(22:24:26) sts.

Leave rem 20(22:24:26) sts on a holder.

LEFT FRONT

With 3.25mm (US 3) needles, cast on 30(32:35:37) sts.

K 7 rows.

Change to 4mm (US 6) needles.

1st row: K to end.

2nd row: K4, p to end.

These 2 rows **set** st st with g st border.

Cont in patt until left front measures 8cm/3¼in from cast-on edge, ending with 2nd row of patt.

SHAPE ARMHOLE

Next row (right side): Cast (bind) off 4 sts, k to end.

26(28:31:33) sts.

Cont in patt until left front measures 14 rows less than back, ending with 2nd row of patt.

SHAPE NECK

Next row (right side): K to last 7(8:9:10) sts, leave these unworked sts on a holder, turn and work on rem 19(20:22:23) sts for side of neck.

Next row: P to end.

Next row: K to last 2 sts, k2tog.

Rep the last 2 rows 4 times more.

14(15:17:18) sts.

Work 3 rows in st st.

SHAPE SHOULDER

Cast (bind) off.

RIGHT FRONT

With 3.25mm (US 3) needles, cast on 30(32:35:37) sts.

K 7 rows.

Change to 4mm (US 6) needles.

1st row: K to end.

2nd row: P to last 4 sts, k4.

These 2 rows **set** st st with g st border.

Cont in patt until right front measures 8cm/3¼in from cast-on edge, ending with 2nd row of patt.

SHAPE ARMHOLE

Next row (right side): K to end.

Next row (wrong side): Cast (bind) off 4 sts, p to last 4 sts, k4.

26(28:31:33) sts.

Buttonhole row: K2, yf, k2tog, k to end.

Cont straight in patt until right front measures 14 rows less than back, ending with 2nd row of patt.

SHAPE NECK

Next row (right side): Break yarn, slip first 7(8:9:10) sts onto a holder, k to end.

19(20:22:23) sts.

Next row: P to end.

Next row: Skpo, k to end.

Rep the last 2 rows 4 times more.

14(15:17:18) sts.

Work 4 rows in st st.

SHAPE SHOULDER

Cast (bind) off.

SLEEVES (MAKE 2)

With 3.25mm (US 3) needles, cast on 33(35:37:39) sts.

K 7 rows.

Change to 4mm (US 6) needles.

Work 4 rows in st st, beginning with a k row.

Increase row: K3, m1, k to last 3 sts, m1, k3.

Work 3 rows in st st.

Rep the last 4 rows 4(5:6:7) times and then rep only increase row once more.

45(49:53:57) sts.

Cont straight in st st until sleeve measures 13(15:17:19) cm/5(6:6¾:7½)in from cast-on edge, ending with a p row.

Place markers at each end of last row.

Work a further 4 rows in st st.

Cast (bind) off.

MAKING UP

Join shoulder seams.

NECKBAND

With right side facing, using 3.25mm (US 3) needles, slip 7(8:9:10) sts from right front neck holder onto right needle, rejoin yarn, pick up and knit 11 sts up right side of front neck, k across 20(22:24:26) sts from back neck holder, pick up and knit 11 sts down left side of front neck, k7(8:9:10) sts from left front holder.

56(60:64:68) sts.

K 1 row.

Buttonhole row: K2, yf, k2tog, k to end.

K 2 rows.

Cast (bind) off knitwise.

TO FINISH

Sew on sleeves into armholes, matching rows above markers to armhole cast-off (bound-off) sts. Join side and sleeve seams. Sew on buttons, matching buttonholes.

Tip

Working yf. k2tog makes a small neat buttonhole which is ideal for baby knits

Tom's Trousers

MEASUREMENTS

TO FIT AGES
0-3 3-6 6-9 9-12 months

FINISHED SIZES
Waist circumference

33	36	40	44 cm
13	14¼	15¾	17¼ in

Length (from centre front)

29	36	43	46 cm
11½	14¼	17	18 in

MATERIALS

Yarn quantities are based on average requirements and are therefore approximate.

- 50g/1¾oz balls of West Yorkshire Spinners Pure DK:
  - 2(3:3:4) balls in River
- Pair of 3.25mm (US 3) knitting needles
- Pair of 4mm (US 6) knitting needles
- 3.25mm (US 3) circular needle, 40cm/16in long
- 4mm (US 6) circular needle, 40cm/16in long
- Elastic thread for waist, optional
- Stitch holders or spare needles
- Stitch marker

TENSION

22 sts and 28 rows to 10cm/4in square over st st using 4mm (US 6) needles.

SPECIAL ABBREVIATIONS

wrap 1 on a k side row: yarn to front, slip next st onto right hand needle, yarn to back, slip st back onto left hand needle, when working across the wrapped st on the next row, work the wrapped st and the wrapping loop tog as one st.

wrap 1 on a p side row: yarn to back, slip next st onto right hand needle, yarn to front, slip st back onto left hand needle, when working across the wrapped st on the next row, work the wrapped st and the wrapping loop tog as one st.

PATTERN NOTE

Trousers are worked from the top down in the round, then separated to work each leg back and forth in rows.

TROUSERS WAIST

With 3.25mm (US3) circular needle, cast on 72(80:88:96) sts. Join to work in the round, being careful not to twist stitches, place marker for beg of round.

1st round: K to end.

2nd round: P to end.

Rep last 2 rounds three times more.

Change to 4mm (US 6) circular needle.

Inc round: [K2, m1] to end.

108(120:132:144) sts.

SHAPE BACK

1st row: K10, wrap 1, turn.

2nd row: P20, wrap 1, turn.

3rd row: K30, wrap 1, turn.

4th row: P40, wrap 1, turn.

5th row: K50, wrap 1, turn.

6th row: P60, wrap 1, turn.

7th row: K70, wrap 1, turn.

8th row: P80, wrap 1, turn.

3RD AND 4TH SIZES ONLY

9th row: K90, wrap 1, turn.

10th row: P100, wrap 1, turn.

ALL SIZES

Next round: K to marker.

Next round: K to end.

Cont to K every round until trousers measure 17(20:23:24)cm/6¾(7¾:9:9½)in from cast-on edge, measuring from front of trousers.

SEPARATE FOR LEGS

Next round: Cast (bind) off 4(4:5:6) sts, k46(52:56:60) sts including st left from casting off, cast off 4(4:5:6) sts, place marker, cast off 4(4:5:6) sts, k46(52:56:60) sts including st left from casting off, cast off rem 4(4:5:6) sts.

46(52:56:60) sts for each leg.

Work each leg separately.

FIRST LEG

Change to 4mm (US 6) knitting needles.

Working on first 46(52:56:60) sts for first leg, working back and forth in rows, cont in st st, beginning with a k row, until leg measures 11(15:19:21) cm/4¼(6:7½:8¼)in from cast (bind) off for leg separation, ending with a k row.

Next row: [P5(6:7:8), p2tog] 6 times, p4(4:2:0).

40(46:50:54) sts.

Change to 3.25mm (US 3) needles.

K 5 rows.

Cast (bind) off knitwise.

SECOND LEG

Work as for first leg to end.

TO FINISH

Join inner leg seams. Optionally thread elastic cord to wrong side of base of waist.

Hooded Blanket

MEASUREMENTS

FINISHED SIZE
Length 50cm/19¾in

Width 50cm/19¾in

MATERIALS

Yarn quantities are based on average requirements and are therefore approximate.

- 50g/1¾oz balls of West Yorkshire Spinners Bo Peep DK:
    - 4 balls in Teddy Bear (A)
    - Small amount of Black
- Pair of 3.75mm (US 5) knitting needles

TENSION

22 sts and 30 rows to 10cm/4in square over st st using 3.75mm (US 5) needles.

CHART NOTES

Colourwork is created by using Swiss darning/duplicate stitch on completion of blanket.

BLANKET

With 3.75mm (US 5) needles and A, cast on 2 sts.

INCREASING SECTION

1st row: [Kfb] twice.

4 sts.

2nd row: K to end.

3rd row: K1, [kfb] twice, k1.

6 sts.

4th row: K to end.

5th row: K1, kfb, k to last 2 sts, kfb, k1.

6th row: K to end.

These last 2 rows **set** inc patt.

Cont in patt for a further 142 rows.

150 sts.

DECREASING SECTION

149th row: K1, skpo, k to last 3 sts, k2tog, k1.

150th row: K to end.

These last 2 rows **set** dec patt.

Cont in patt for a further 144 rows.

4 sts.

295th row: Skpo, k2tog.

2 sts.

296th row: K to end.

297th row: Skpo and fasten off.

HOOD

With 3.75mm (US 5) needles and A, cast on 2 sts.

INCREASING SECTION

1st row: [Kfb] twice.

4 sts.

2nd row: K to end.

3rd row: K1, [kfb] twice, k1.

6 sts.

4th row: K2, p2, k2.

5th row: K1, kfb, k to last 2 sts, kfb, k1.

6th row: K2, p to last 2 sts, k2.

These last 2 rows **set** inc patt.

Cont in patt for 15 rows.

24 sts.

SHAPE EARS

22nd row: K2, p to last 2 sts, k2, cast on 12 sts.

36 sts.

23rd row: K13, kfb, k to last 2 sts, kfb, k1, cast on 12 sts.

50 sts.

24th row: K14, p22, k14.

25th row: K1, skpo, k10, kfb, k to last 14 sts, kfb, k10, k2tog, k1.

26th row: K13, p24, k13.

27th row: K1, skpo, k9, kfb, k to last 13 sts, kfb, k9, k2tog, k1.

28th row: K12, p26, k12.

CHART ONE

KEY
☐ A
■ Black

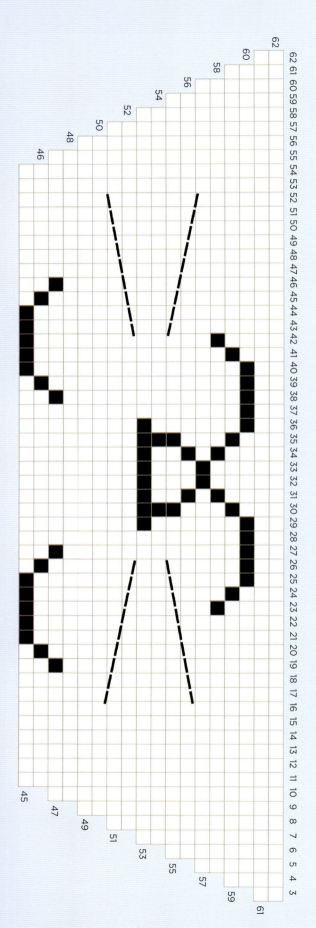

29th row: K1, skpo, k8, kfb, k to last 12 sts, kfb, k8, k2tog, k1.

30th row: K11, p28, k11.

31st row: K1, skpo, k7, kfb, k to last 11 sts, kfb, k7, k2tog, k1.

32nd row: K10, p30, k10.

33rd row: K1, skpo, k6, kfb, k to last 10 sts, kfb, k6, k2tog, k1.

34th row: K9, p32, k9.

35th row: K1, skpo, k5, kfb, k to last 9 sts, kfb, k5, k2tog, k1.

36th row: K8, p34, k8.

37th row: K1, skpo, k4, kfb, k to last 8 sts, kfb, k4, k2tog, k1.

38th row: K7, p36, k7.

39th row: K1, skpo, k3, kfb, k to last 7 sts, kfb, k3, k2tog, k1.

40th row: K6, p38, k6.

41st row: K1, skpo, k2, kfb, k to last 6 sts, kfb, k2, k2tog, k1.

42nd row: K5, p40, k5.

43rd row: K1, skpo, k1, kfb, k to last 5 sts, kfb, k1, k2tog, k1.

44th row: K4, p42, k4.

45th row: K1, skpo, kfb, k to last 4 sts, kfb, k2tog, k1.

46th row: K3, p44, k3.

47th row: K to end.

48th row: K2, p to last 2 sts, k2.

50 sts.

LOWER HOOD

49th row: K1, kfb, k to last 2 sts, kfb, k1.

50th row: K2, p to last 2 sts, k2.

These last 2 rows **set** inc patt.

Cont in inc patt for 12 more rows.

64 sts.

63rd row: K1, kfb, k to last 2 sts, kfb, k1.

64th row: K to end.

Rep last 2 rows once more.

68 sts.

67th row: K1, kfb, k to last 2 sts, kfb, k1.

70 sts.

Cast (bind) off knitwise.

TO FINISH

With right side facing, using Black and chart one for placement, working on st st section of hood from 45th–62nd rows, add cat face to hood by working Swiss darning/duplicate stitch.

Using back stitch and Black, embroider whiskers either side of nose.

Attach hood to cast-on corner of blanket.

Kitten Ears Cap

MEASUREMENTS

TO FIT AGES
0–3   3–6   6–12 months

MATERIALS

Yarn quantities are based on average requirements and are therefore approximate.

- 50g/1¾oz balls of West Yorkshire Spinners Bo Peep DK:
  - 1(1:2) ball(s) in Sparkle
- Pair of 3.25mm (US 3) knitting needles
- Pair of 4mm (US 6) knitting needles

SPECIAL ABBREVIATIONS

wrap 1 on a k side row: yarn to front, slip next st onto right hand needle, yarn to back, slip st back onto left hand needle, when working across the wrapped st on the next row, work the wrapped st and the wrapping loop tog as one st.

wrap 1 on a p side row: yarn to back, slip next st onto right hand needle, yarn to front, slip st back onto left hand needle, when working across the wrapped st on the next row, work the wrapped st and the wrapping loop tog as one st.

TENSION

22 sts and 28 rows to 10cm/4in square over st st using 4mm (US 6) needles.

CAP

With 3.25mm (US 3) needles cast on 55(61:67) sts.

K 3 rows.

Change 4mm (US 6) needles.

Work 12 rows in st st, beginning with a k row.

FIRST EAR

13th row: K24(26:28), wrap 1, turn.

**

14th row: P15, wrap 1, turn.

15th row: K14, wrap 1, turn.

16th row: P13, wrap 1, turn.

17th row: K12, wrap 1, turn.

18th row: P11, wrap 1, turn.

19th row: K10, wrap 1, turn.

20th row: P9, wrap 1, turn.

21st row: K8, wrap 1, turn.

22nd row: P7, wrap 1, turn.

23rd row: K6, wrap 1, turn.

24th row: P5, wrap 1, turn.

25th row: K4, wrap 1, turn.

26th row: P3, wrap 1, turn.

27th row: K2, wrap 1, turn.

Working previously wrapped sts together with loops as you work them, cont as follows.

28th row: P3, wrap 1, turn.

29th row: K4, wrap 1, turn.

30th row: P5, wrap 1, turn.

31st row: K6, wrap 1, turn.

32nd row: P7, wrap 1, turn.

33rd row: K8, wrap 1, turn.

34th row: P9, wrap 1, turn.

35th row: K10, wrap 1, turn.

36th row: P11, wrap 1, turn.

37th row: K12, wrap 1, turn.

38th row: P13, wrap 1, turn.

39th row: K14, wrap 1, turn.

40th row: P to end.

***

SECOND EAR

41st row: K to last 9(11:13) sts, wrap 1, turn.

Rep from ** to *** once more.

Cont in st st (throughout), beginning with a k row, work 12(14:16) rows.

SHAPE BACK

Next row: [K4, k2tog] to last st, k1.

46(51:56) sts.

Next row: P to end.

Next row: [K3, k2tog] to last st, k1.

37(41:45) sts.

Next row: P to end.

Next row: [K2, k2tog] to last st, k1.

28(31:34) sts.

Next row: P to end.

Next row: [K1, k2tog] to last st, k1.

19(21:23) sts.

Next row: P to end.

Next row: [K2tog] to last st, k1.

10(11:12) sts.

Leaving a long end, break yarn and thread through rem sts, pull up and secure.

MAKING UP

Join back seam from fasten-off edge to beg of shape back.

EDGING

With right side facing, using 3.25mm (US 3) needles, pick up and knit 25(26:28) sts along each side edge of cap.

50(52:56) sts.

K 5 rows.

Cast (bind) off knitwise.

Techniques

Sometimes on adventures you need a helping hand, such as when Thomasina Tittlemouse helps the Flopsy Bunnies escape from the farmer's sack.

This section contains a bit of guidance for techniques used in this book, including basic and intermediate knitting skills, casting on and off, seaming with mattress stitch, colourwork, and creating texture.

BASIC SKILLS

SLIP KNOT

This knot attaches the yarn to the needle.

Make a loop in the yarn near the end (A). Bring the ball-end of the yarn under the loop and use the tip of the needle to pull it to the front (B).

Pull both ends of the yarn to secure the knot around the needle. Do not pull too tightly, leave the slip knot slightly loose (C).

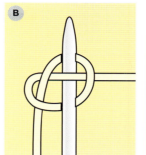
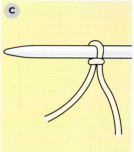

THUMB CAST ON

This method creates an elastic edge suitable for stitches or yarns without much stretch.

Measure out about 2.5cm/1in of yarn for each stitch to be made. Make a slip knot on the left hand needle at the end of the measured yarn.

Holding the needle and the ball-end of the yarn in the right hand, wrap the cut end around the thumb (A). Insert the tip of the right hand needle up through the loop on the thumb (B). Wrap the cut end of the yarn around the needle (C) and pull a loop through to form a stitch on the needle (D).

Drop the loop on the thumb and pull the yarn to tighten the stitch on the needle. Repeat these steps until you have the required number of stitches.

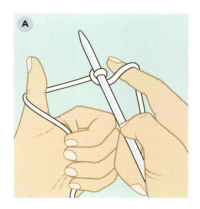
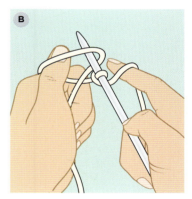
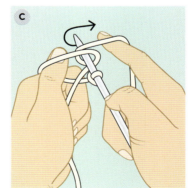
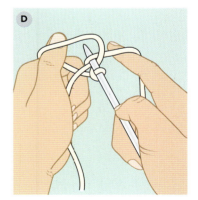

Techniques

CABLE CAST ON

This method creates a firm edge that is not particularly elastic.

Begin with a slip knot on the needle. Hold the needle with slip knot in your left hand and insert the tip of the needle in your right hand into the slip knot, from front to back.

Take the ball end of the yarn under the left hand needle and over the right hand needle (A). Draw it through the slip knot with the tip of the right hand needle to make the first stitch (B). Slide the new stitch onto the left hand needle (C). To make more stitches, slide the right hand needle between the two stitches on the left hand needle from front to back, wrap the yarn around the tip of the right hand needle as before (D). Draw a loop through and place the new stitch on the left hand needle. Repeat until you have the required number of stitches.

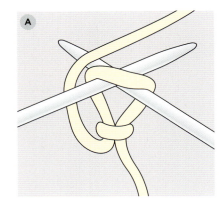

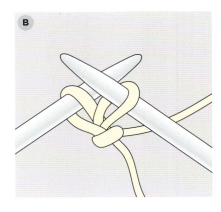

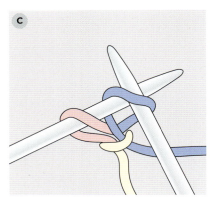

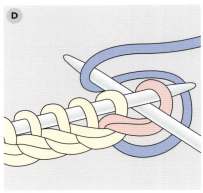

KNIT STITCH (K)

Hold the needle with the stitches in your left hand, with the yarn at the back. Insert the tip of the right hand needle into the first stitch from front to back and left to right (A).

Take the yarn under and around the right hand needle from left to right (B). Use the tip of the right hand needle to pull the loop through the stitch on the left hand needle to form a new stitch on the right hand needle (C).

Slide off the stitch on the left hand needle (D).

Repeat these steps to the end of the row.

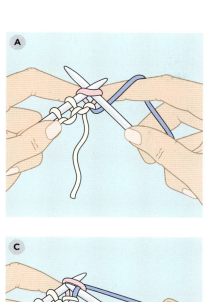
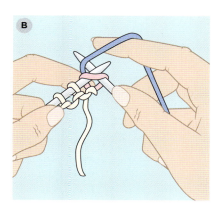
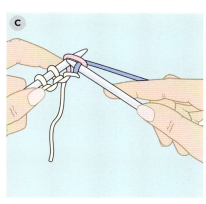
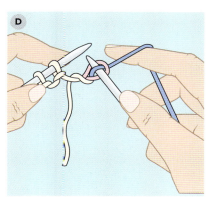

PURL STITCH (P)

Hold the needle with the stitches in your left hand, with the yarn at the front. Insert the tip of the right hand needle into the first stitch from right to left (A).

Take the yarn over and around the right hand needle to form the next stitch (B). Use the tip of the right hand needle to pull the loop through the stitch on the left hand needle to form a new stitch on the right hand needle (C).

Slide off the stitch on the left hand needle (D).

Repeat these steps to the end of the row.

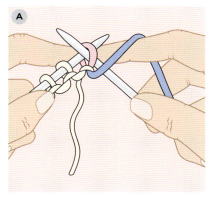
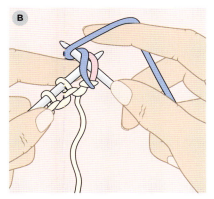
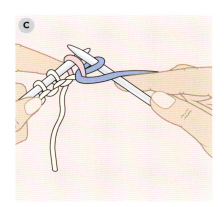
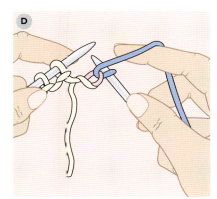

SLIP STITCH

Purlwise (A): insert the right hand needle from right to left (as if to purl a stitch) into the next stitch on the left hand needle and move it from left to right needle.

Knitwise (B): insert the right hand needle from left to right (as if to knit a stitch) into the next stitch on the left hand needle and move it from left to right needle.

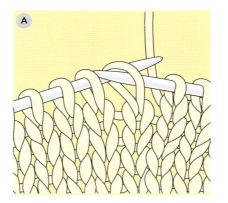
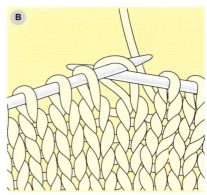

CAST (BIND) OFF

Casting (binding) off can be done knitwise or purlwise, or following a pattern such as in rib.

To cast (bind) off knitwise, knit the first stitch, then knit a second stitch. Insert the tip of the left hand needle into the first stitch (A) and lift it over the second (B) to cast off the first stitch (C). Knit the next stitch and then lift the previous stitch over it. Repeat until the row is cast (bound) off and there is just one stitch left. Break the yarn, thread it through the final stitch and tighten.

To cast (bind) off purlwise, work the same way as for knitwise but purl the stitches instead of knitting them.

To cast (bind) off in rib, work the same way as for knitwise but knit all knit stitches and purl all purl stitches.

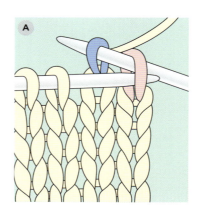
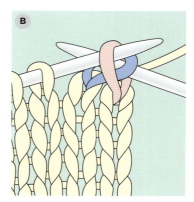
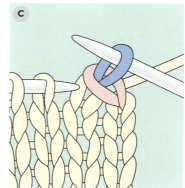
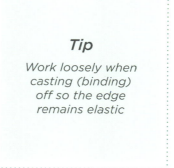

Tip

Work loosely when casting (binding) off so the edge remains elastic

DECREASES

KNIT TWO STITCHES TOGETHER (K2TOG)

This decreases by knitting two stitches together and makes a right-slanting decrease on the right side of stocking stitch (stockinette).

Insert the tip of the right hand needle into the next two stitches from left to right and knit them as one stitch.

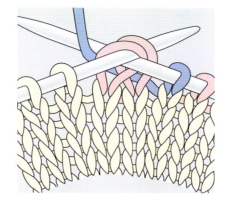

PURL TWO STITCHES TOGETHER (P2TOG)

This decreases by purling two stitches together and makes a right-slanting decrease on the wrong side of stocking stitch (stockinette).

Insert the tip of the right hand needle into the next two stitches from right to left and purl them as one stitch.

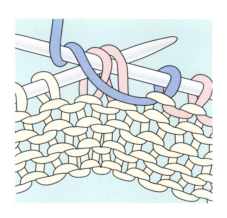

Tip

K2tog and p2tog always slant to the right on the right side of the fabric

SLIP ONE, KNIT ONE, PASS SLIPPED STITCH OVER (SKPO)

This decreases by one stitch and makes a left-slanting decrease on the right side of stocking stitch (stockinette).

Slip the first stitch knitwise and knit the second stitch (A). Then pass the slipped stitch over the knitted stitch (B) and off the needle.

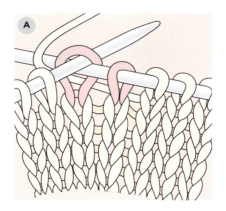
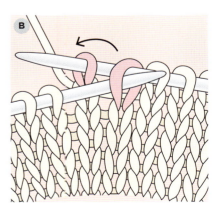

Techniques

SLIP ONE, KNIT TWO TOGETHER, PASS SLIPPED STITCH OVER (SL1, K2TOG, PSSO)

This decreases by two stitches at a time.

Slip the first stitch knitwise onto the right hand needle (A) and then knit the next two stitches together (B). Pass the slipped stitch over the two stitches knitted together (C) and off the needle.

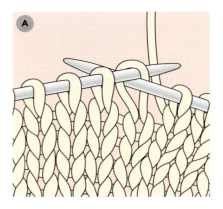
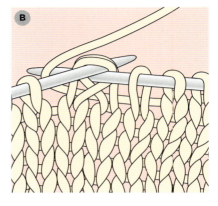
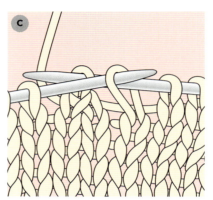

Tip

This is called a double decrease because it reduces three stitches to only one stitch (decreasing two stitches together). The remaining stitch slants to the left

INCREASES

KNIT FRONT AND BACK (KFB)

This is a basic method of increasing one stitch knitwise.

Insert the tip of the right hand needle into the next stitch on the left hand needle and knit it in the usual way but do not slip it off the needle. Insert the tip of the right hand needle into the back of the same stitch on the left hand needle, take the yarn forward and knit the stitch again. Now slip the original stitch off the left hand needle.

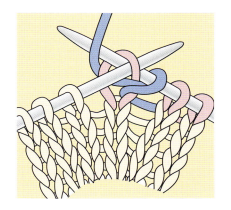

Tip

This increase will show as a bar across the base of the second stitch

MAKE ONE STITCH (M1)

This technique will increase one stitch knitwise and makes a left-slanting increase on the right side of stocking stitch (stockinette).

Pick up bar between two stitches from front to back (A) and place on the left hand needle. Knit into the back loop (B).

To work m1 purlwise, pick up bar from back to front and purl through the front loop.

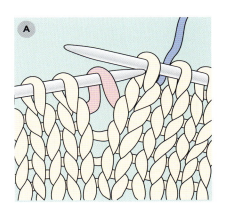
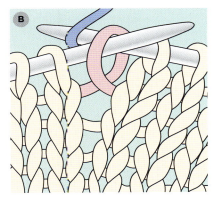

EYELET INCREASE KNITWISE YARN FORWARD (YF)

This increase creates one stitch with an eyelet underneath.

Knit to the eyelet position, bring the yarn forward between the needles and then over the needle to the back again before knitting the next stitch.

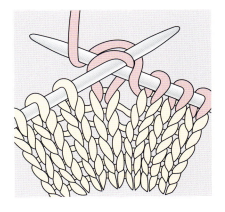

INTERMEDIATE SKILLS

PICK UP STITCHES

This technique is shown here along the cast-off (bound-off) edge, but the principle is the same on any edge.

With the right side of the work facing you, insert the point of the knitting needle from the front to back into the knitted fabric at the point where you want to start picking up from. Loop the yarn around the point of the needle (A) and draw the loop through to the front to form a new stitch (B).

Continue in this way along the edge to pick up as many stitches as instructed (C).

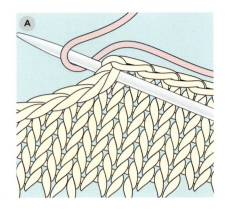

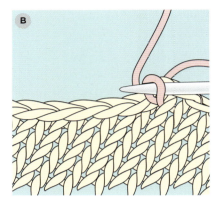

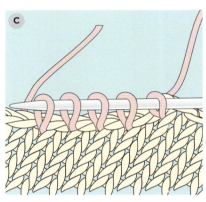

Tip
Work carefully and pick up the stitches evenly along the edge

USING A CIRCULAR NEEDLE

Using your preferred cast-on method, cast on to one of the points of the needle the amount of stitches instructed and spread out the cast-on stitches along the 2 needles and the cable that joins them.

Before joining to make a round check that cast-on edge is not twisted or the whole piece of knitting will be permanently twisted.

The first stitch in the first round is the beginning of the round and all following rounds start in the same position. To keep track of the rounds, place a marker on the needle.

Knit the stitches from the right hand point of the needle to the left hand point, sliding around the cable as you work. When you get back to the marker, you have completed one round.

I-CORD

This creates a "tube" of knitting.

Cast on as many stitches as instructed.

*Slide the stitches to the right-hand end of the needle, with the working yarn on the left of the cast-on row. Pull the yarn tightly across the back of the stitches and knit the first stitch as firmly as you can, then knit the remaining stitches.

Repeat from * until the I-cord is the length you need.

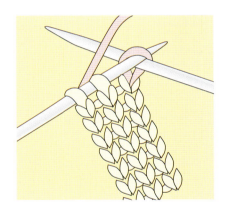

Tip

I-cord has many uses, including applied as an embellishment — see for example the stalk on the Squirrel Nutkin Acorn Hat

COLOURWORK

FAIR ISLE/STRANDED COLOURWORK

On a knit row, knit the stitches in first colour to the colour change, join in second colour leaving tail at the back of work, knit in second colour to next colour change, drop second colour and pick up first colour, bringing it across under the strand of second colour to wrap around the needle (A), making sure not to pull too tight.

Knit the stitches in first colour; when you change back to second colour bring it across over the strand of first colour (B) and continue in this way.

On a purl row, purl the stitches in first colour; at the colour change, drop first colour and pick up second colour, bringing it across under the strand of first colour, to wrap around the needle (C), making sure not to pull too tight.

Purl the stitches in second colour, when you change back to first colour, bring it across over the strand of second colour (D) and continue in this way.

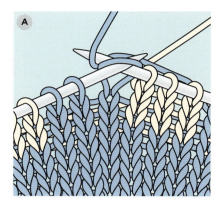
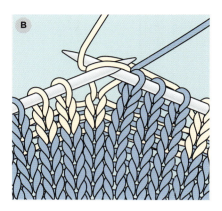
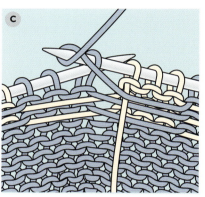
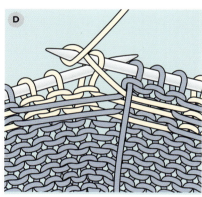

INTARSIA

On a knit row, work to the last stitch of the first colour, bring the second colour under the first colour (A) and knit the next stitch firmly to secure.

On a purl row, work to the last stitch of the first colour, bring the second colour under the first colour (B) and purl the next stitch firmly to secure.

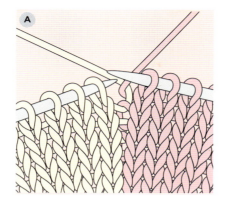
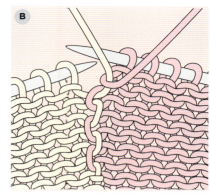

SWISS DARNING/ DUPLICATE STITCH

Thread a tapestry (darning) needle with the yarn in the same weight used to knit with. From the back, bring the needle out from the base of a knitted stitch to be embroidered (A). Pass the needle around the top of the stitch, going under the 'legs' of the stitch above (B).

Insert the needle back through the base of the same stitch to cover the knitted stitch below (C). Bring the needle through at the base of the next stitch and repeat (D).

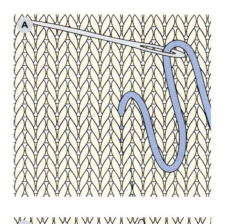
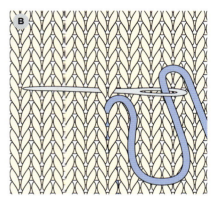
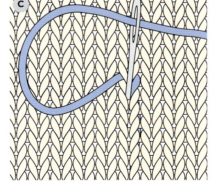
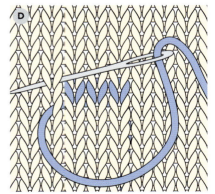

CREATING TEXTURE

RIB (K1, P1 RIB)

Rib is formed by alternately knitting and purling stitches, to create strong vertical lines. Wider vertical lines can be made by working pairs of stitches, called k2, p2 rib. Rib creates a very elastic fabric with horizontal stretch.

*Knit the first stitch (A), then purl the second stitch (B). Repeat from * to end of the row. On the next row, purl the knit stitches and knit the purl stitches, and continue alternating on following rows. When changing from knit to purl, take the yarn between the stitches not over the needle.

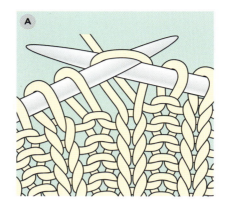
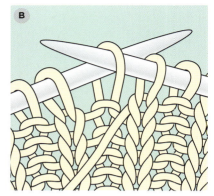

CABLE STITCH (C4B AND C4F)

C4B: Work to the position of the cable. Slip the next two stitches from the left hand needle onto the cable needle. Move the cable needle and stitches to the back of the work (A). Knit the next two stitches from the left hand needle (B), then knit the two stitches from the cable needle to complete the cable.

C4F: Work to the position of the cable. Slip the next two stitches from the left hand needle onto the cable needle. Move the cable needle and stitches to the front of the work (C). Knit the next two stitches from the left hand needle (D), then knit the two stitches from the cable needle to complete the cable.

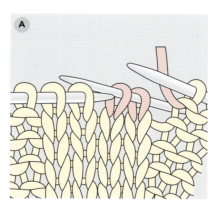
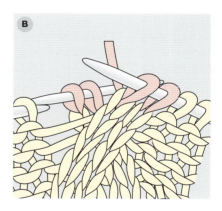
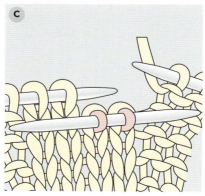
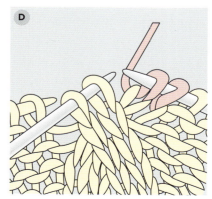

TWIST STITCH (TW2R)

Put the right hand needle into the back of the second stitch on the left hand needle and knit it through the back loop (A). But do not drop the original stitch off the left hand needle.

Then put the right hand needle knitwise into the first stitch on the left hand needle and knit into it (B). Drop both original stitches off the left hand needle to complete the twist.

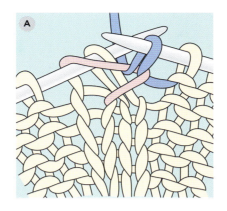
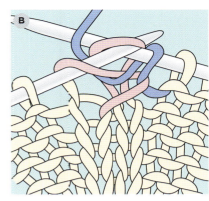

BOBBLE STITCH

Work to the position of the bobble. Knit, then purl, then knit, then purl into the next stitch. Taking the yarn to the back and front as needed to make stitches. Then drop the original stitch off the left hand needle. Increasing one stitch to four stitches (A).

Turn the work and purl the four bobble stitches (B).

Turn the work again and knit the four bobble stitches. Then turn the work and purl the stitches again; three rows of stocking stitch (stockinette) have been worked on the bobble stitches (C).

Turn the work so that the right side is facing. K2tog twice, slip the first k2tog over the second and off the needle to complete the bobble (D).

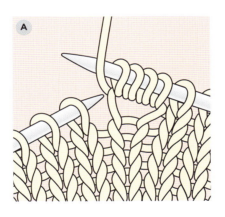
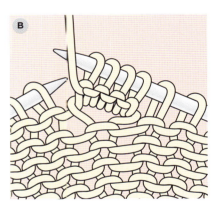
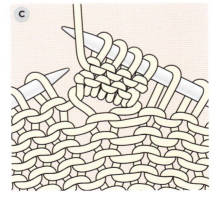
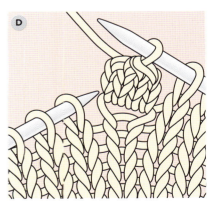

SEAMING

MATTRESS STITCH: STOCKING STITCH (STOCKINETTE) ROW ENDS

With right sides facing, lay the two edges to be joined side by side. Thread a blunt tip sewing needle with a long length of yarn and secure the yarn on the back of the right hand knitted piece. Bring the needle up from the back between the first and second stitch of that piece and immediately above the cast-on edge. Take it across to the left hand piece and from the back bring it through between the first and second stitches of that piece, immediately above the cast-on edge. Take it back to right hand piece and bring it up one row above where it first came through between the first and second stitches and pull through. Take the needle across to the left hand piece, and bring it up one row above where it first came through between the first and second stitches and pull through. Continue in the same way working up one row at a time. When you have sewn about 3cm/1¼in gently pull the stitches up to close the seam.

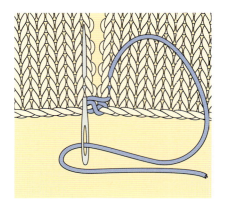

MATTRESS STITCH: GARTER STITCH ROW ENDS

Use the same technique as for seaming stocking stitch row ends. Take the needle under the lower loop on each ridge on one knitted piece, and under the upper loop on each ridge on the other piece.

Tip

Don't pull too tightly as it should look like a continuation of the stitch pattern

MATTRESS STITCH: MOSS STITCH ROW ENDS

Use the same technique as for seaming stocking stitch row ends, and take the needle between the first and second stitches on each piece, and under only one bar of yarn on each piece to work up one row at a time.

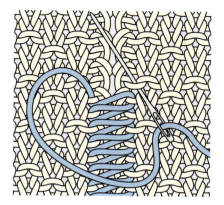

Tip

Make sure you are always working into the same column of stitches on each side of the seam as you work

MATTRESS STITCH: CAST-OFF (BOUND-OFF) EDGES

With right sides facing, lay the pieces to be joined edge to edge. Thread a blunt tip sewing needle with a long length of yarn and secure the yarn on the back of the lower knitted piece, then bring the needle up through the middle of the first whole stitch. Take the needle under both loops of the first whole stitch on the upper piece, so that it emerges between the first and second stitches.

Go back into the lower piece, taking the needle through to the back of where is first came out, and then bring it back to the front in the middle of the next stitch along. Pull the yarn through.

Take the needle under both loops of the next whole stitch on the upper piece (A). Continue in the same way working along one column of stitches at a time.

When you have sewn about 3cm/1¼in (B), gently pull the stitches up to close the seam.

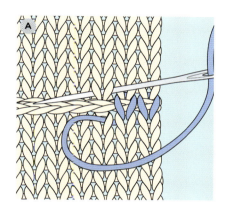

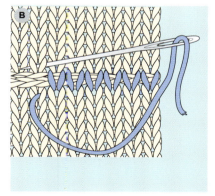

ABOUT THE AUTHOR

Debbie Bliss studied Fashion and Textiles at art school in London, specialising in knitwear. After graduating she became known for her knitted plants which were sold in stores such as Liberty of London. She has published over 40 books on fashion knits and babywear and lectured at prestigious venues such as the Royal Ontario Museum and the Fashion and Textile Museum in London. In 2000 she launched a highly successful range of luxury hand knit yarns which are sold globally. One of her favourite paintings is the portrait of Beatrix Potter by Delmar Banner which hangs in the National Gallery in London.

In 2015 she was awarded an MBE for her contribution to knitting and the craft industry.

ACKNOWLEDGEMENTS

This book wouldn't have been possible without the support of the following amazing people:

Ame Verso for commissioning the book and being encouraging, patient and enthusiastic.

Sarah Rowntree for her perfect styling of the layettes.

Chloé Birch for her invaluable support in pattern compiling and production and for her creative input.

Sam Staddon for the beautiful layouts.

Jason Jenkins for the great photography.

Thomas Merrington for his guidance and insight into the Peter Rabbit brand.

Jessica Cropper, my editor, for her overview and skill in keeping everything on track.

Tricia Gilbert, the project editor, for her technical input as she guided me through the labyrinth of patterns and charts.

Helen Birch for casting her wise eye on the initial patterns.

Rosy Tucker for charts that brought the characters to life.

SUPPLIERS

Debbie Bliss yarns are available online at Lovecrafts.com and Yarn.com. and in store at WEBS, 75 Service Center Rd, Northampton, MA 01060, USA, yarn.com

For stockists of West Yorkshire Spinners Bo Peep Luxury Baby DK and Pure DK contact westyorkshirespinners.com

INDEX

abbreviations 10
acorn designs 72, 75–9
armholes 61, 88–9, 90, 98, 100

Beanie, Bunny Ears 32–3
blankets
    Hooded 104–7
    Mrs Tiggy-Winkle™ 82–6
    Owl Island 70–7
    Patchwork 27–31
    Puddle-duck 40–7
bobble stitch 123
Bonnet, Embroidered 48–9
booties
    Duck Beak 56–7
    Radish 34–5
borders 46, 82, 84, 86
Bunny Ears Beanie 32–3
button/buttonhole bands 55

cable cast on 112
cable stitch 122
cable tree square 76, 77
Cap, Kitten Ears 108–9
Capelet, Flopsy™ 36–7
cardigans
    Gingham 87–90
    Jemima 50–5
    Kitten 98–101
cast (bind) off 114
cast on
    cable 112
    thumb 111
cast-off edges 125
charts, reading 11
colourwork 120–1
Cotton-tail™ 18–37

decreases 104, 115–16
duplicate stitch 121

edging 46, 49, 84, 86, 109
eyelet increase knitwise yarn forward 117

Fair Isle 77, 120
Flopsy™ 18–37
    Capelet 36–7

garment care 13
garter stitch row ends 124
gingham 84, 87–90

hats 32–3, 48–9, 78–9, 108–9
Hooded Blanket 104–7

I-cord 119
increases 100, 104, 117
intarsia 121

Jacket, Nutkin 64–9
Jemima Puddle-duck™ 38–57
    Duck Beak Booties 56–7
    Embroidered Bonnet 48–9
    Jemima Cardigan 50–5
    Puddle-duck Blanket 40–7

knit front and back 117
knit stitch 113
knit two stitches together 115
knitting needles 14–15
    circular 14, 119
    double-pointed 14
    sizes 15
    straight 14

leaf designs 72, 77, 79

make one stitch 117
materials 8, 12–13
mattress stitch 124, 124–5
measurements 8
Mopsy™ 18–37
moss stitch row ends 125
Mrs Tiggy-Winkle™ 80–95
    Gingham Cardigan 87–90
    Hedgehog Rattle 94–5
    Hedgehog Shoes 91–3
    Mrs Tiggy-Winkle™ Blanket 82–6
mushroom patterns 72, 74

necks 24, 26, 36, 53, 54, 62, 98, 100–1

Owl Island Blanket 70–7

patchwork 20–6, 27–31
patterns, reading 8–10
Peter Rabbit™ 18–37
    Bunny Ears Beanie 32–3
    Flopsy™ Capelet 36–7
    Patchwork Blanket 27–31
    Patchwork Sweater 20–6
    Radish Booties 34–5
pick up stitches 118
pom-poms 17, 30
purl stitch 113
purl two stitches together 115

radish designs 25, 34–5
Rattle, Hedgehog 94–5
rib 122
row ends 124–5

safety issues 11
seaming 124–5
Shoes
    Hedgehog 91–3
    see also booties
shoulders 53, 88–9, 90, 98, 100
sizes 8
sleeves 26, 54, 62, 90, 98, 100
    raglan 67–8
slip knots 111
slip one, knit one, pass slipped stitch over 115
slip one, knit two together, pass slipped stitch over 116
slip stitch 114
Squirrel Nutkin™ 58–79
    Acorn Hat 78–9
    Acorn Yoke Sweater 60–3
    Nutkin Jacket 64–9
    Owl Island Blanket 70–7
stocking stitch row ends 124
stranded colourwork 120
straps 93
sweaters
    Acorn Yoke 60–3
    Patchwork 20–6
Swiss darning stitch 121

techniques 110–25
tension (gauge) 9
texture 122–3
ties, cardigan 90
Tom Kitten™ 96–109
    Hooded Blanket 104–7
    Kitten Cardigan 98–101
    Kitten Ears Cap 108–9
    Tom's Trousers 102–3
tools 14–17
Trousers, Tom's 102–3
twist stitch 123

waists, trouser 102

yarns 8, 12–13
yokes 62–3

A DAVID AND CHARLES BOOK

BEATRIX POTTER™, PETER RABBIT™
© Frederick Warne & Co., 2025. All rights reserved.

Frederick Warne & Co. is the owner of all rights, copyrights and trademarks in the Beatrix Potter character names and illustrations.

Licensed by Frederick Warne & Co.

David and Charles is an imprint of David and Charles, Ltd , Suite A, Tourism House, Pynes Hill, Exeter, EX2 5WS

First published in the UK and USA in 2025

Debbie Bliss has asserted her right to be identified as author of this work in accordance with the Copyright, Designs and Patents Act, 1988.

All rights reserved. No part of this publication may be reproduced in any form or by any means, electronic or mechanical, by photocopying, recording or otherwise, without prior permission in writing from the publisher.

No part of this book may be used or reproduced in any manner for the purpose of training artificial intelligence technologies or systems without permission from David and Charles Ltd.

Readers are permitted to reproduce any of the designs in this book for their personal use and without the prior permission of the publisher. However, the designs in this book are copyright and must not be reproduced for resale.

The author and publisher have made every effort to ensure that all the instructions in the book are accurate and safe, and therefore cannot accept liability for any resulting injury, damage or loss to persons or property, however it may arise.

Names of manufacturers and product ranges are provided for the information of readers, with no intention to infringe copyright or trademarks.

A catalogue record for this book is available from the British Library.

ISBN-13: 9781446315828 paperback
ISBN-13: 9781446315842 EPUB

This book has been printed on paper from approved suppliers and made from pulp from sustainable sources.

Printed in China through Asia Pacific Offset for:
David and Charles, Ltd , Suite A, Tourism House, Pynes Hill, Exeter, EX2 5WS

10 9 8 7 6 5 4 3 2 1

Publishing Director: Ame Verso
Publishing Manager: Jeni Chown
Editor: Jessica Cropper
Tech Editor: Helen Birch
Pattern Compiling & Hand Knit Production: Chloé Elizabeth Birch
Project Editor: Tricia Gilbert
Design: Sam Staddon
Pre-press Designer: Susan Reansbury
Technical Illustrations: Kuo Kang Chen
Art Direction: Sarah Rowntree
Photography: Jason Jenkins
Production Manager: Beverley Richardson

David and Charles publishes high-quality books on a wide range of subjects. For more information visit www.davidandcharles.com.

Share your makes with us on social media using #dandcbooks and follow us on Facebook and Instagram by searching for @dandcbooks.

Layout of the digital edition of this book may vary depending on reader hardware and display settings.

 BEATRIX POTTER™ © Frederick Warne & Co., 2025. Frederick Warne & Co. is the owner of all rights, copyrights and trademarks in the Beatrix Potter character names and illustrations. Licensed by Frederick Warne & Co. Ltd. All Rights Reserved.